ROOTS *and* WINGS

ROOTS *and* WINGS

DISCOVERING AND DEVELOPING FAMILY STRENGTHS

Karen Lawrence Allen
Gary Gene Allen

THE PILGRIM PRESS
CLEVELAND, OHIO

The Pilgrim Press, Cleveland, Ohio 44115
© 1992 by The Pilgrim Press

Printed in the United States of America
The paper used in this publication is acid free and meets the minimum
requirements of American National Standard for Information Sciences-
Permanence of Paper for Printed Library Materials, ANSI Z39.48-1984

97   96   95   5   4   3   2

Library of Congress Cataloging-in-Publication Data

Allen, Karen Lawrence, 1942-
    Roots and wings : discovering and developing family strengths /
Karen Lawrence Allen, Gary Allen.
        p.   cm.
    Includes bibliographical references.
    ISBN 0-8298-0928-7 (acid-free paper)
    1. Parenting.   2. Family.   I. Allen, Gary, 1942-   . II. Title.
HQ755.8.A46   1992   92-31646
649'.1—dc20   CIP

To our parents,
Ruth and Wayne Lawrence Sr.
and Evelyn and Paul Davis,
who made it all possible,
with love and appreciation

For our children,
Lisa (and husband David),
Christopher, and Timothy,
who make it all worthwhile,
with hope, confidence,
and of course,
as always,
with love

A wise woman once said to me that there are only two lasting bequests we can hope to give our children. One of these she said is roots, the other, wings. And they can only be grown, these roots and wings, in the home.

Hodding Carter, Sr.

"It's How We Like It," from *Where Main Street Meets the River*. Copyright © 1953 by Hodding Carter. Reprinted by permission of Brandt & Brandt, Literary Agents, Inc.

Contents

Acknowledgments _____

We want to give special thanks to friends who were members of the Family Forum class at Foundry United Methodist Church, Washington, D.C., for their inspiration and encouragement as we developed the ideas that led to this book. We also want to thank those who reviewed the early drafts of the manuscript for the benefit of their expertise and comments, especially Phyllis Larsen, Luise Gray, and Adele Hutchins. Thanks, too, to our daughter, Lisa Allen Belk, whose journalistic skills helped us with structure and style. We especially appreciated the work of Marguerite Dobrosielski and Linda Grimm, who typed early drafts of the manuscript, and to Margo Vollmer, whose expertise in WordPerfect helped us survive the corrections and rewrites. Finally, we want to thank The Pilgrim Press for believing in *Roots and Wings*.

1

The Crosswinds
of Change

ROOTS AND WINGS

Roots and Wings is a book about family strengths and how families today, caught in the crosswinds of change, can discover their own strengths and develop additional ones. It is a book about what parents can give to their children and what they can help their children become. For if what Hodding Carter wrote is true and roots and wings are the only lasting bequests parents can leave to children, then perhaps parents should be much more intentional about planning the content of that legacy. Many parents spend more time and thought selecting their children's wardrobes, choosing their preschools, and deciding on colleges than they do thinking about the kind of people they hope their children will become. *Roots and Wings* challenges parents to give priority to the circumstances that shape family life and help build character in children. The roots are provided by the parents and experienced by the children who participate in the sharing, caring, learning, and relating of living together. Wings develop gradually and require the children's responses as they acquire competence and confidence and receive encouragement to do things themselves.

A FRAMEWORK FOR FAMILY STRENGTH

This book will explore roots and wings in the context of a framework for building strength in families. This framework identifies factors that contribute to family strength and invites parents to fill in the blanks by applying these factors to their own situations. These factors are: cohesion (what families share), affection (how parents care), control (why parents teach), and affiliation (who can help).

This chapter explores the changing circumstances affecting families today.

Chapter 2, "Cohesion," describes what the family has in common and what holds it together as a means of building strength. This includes shared activities, rituals and traditions, family conversations, commitment, and—most significantly—values.

In Chapter 3, "Affection," we address feelings in the family and ways of helping children feel valued, valuable, liked, and loved. We also explore ways to help children develop competence, confidence, and self-worth.

Chapter 4, "Control," acknowledges that parenting requires a balance between protection and preparation, permission and accountability, restraint and relinquishment. Recognizing that childhood is a progression along a continuum from parental control to self-control, the chapter helps parents understand how their leadership and discipline can help children make that trip.

Chapter 5, "Affiliation," demonstrates how families who develop outside relationships with other individuals, groups, and institutions can use these ties to help give their families a sense of identification, an assurance of support, and opportunities for perspective and participation.

In each area, the parents first provide and the child receives. Then, as the child participates, the parents protect and teach. Finally, the child initiates and the parents permit and encourage. These roots and wings are what growing up is all about, and—as Hodding Carter's wise woman reminds us—"they can only be grown in the home."

NUMBERS THAT TELL STORIES

Families today are often unable to reconcile conflicting claims on their time, attitudes, affection, and priorities. After all, this is a time in our nation's history when building strong families is seen as the remedy for many of the problems being experienced in society—from drug and alcohol abuse to teen pregnancies, from child abuse to the education crisis in our schools and violence on our streets. Yet this is also a time when many of the traditional supports that families in the past depended upon are

Family Strengths

	Cohesion (sharing)	Affection (caring)	Control (teaching)	Affiliation (relating)
Roots (provided)	experiences traditions rituals	feelings talking doing waiting listening laughing forgiving	inner space outer space continuum	family ties models bridges
Wings (owned)	commitment character values	self-image confidence competence	self-control responsibility accountability	participation support perspective identification

less frequently present. These supports include extended families, fathers present in the home, respected authority figures in the community, values reinforced in the schools, and faith communities that are widely supported by family involvement.

The changes that have taken place in the United States over the past several decades have been so relentless and dramatic that many parents today lack models for addressing them. Neither has society been able to create the support structures to meet all the needs these changes have wrought.[1]

In 1970, 12 percent of the nation's children lived with only one parent, usually the mother. Twenty years later, that number has more than doubled.[2] If current trends continue, more than half of these children will spend part of their growing-up years in a single-parent setting. Indeed, in the United States half of all marriages are expected to end in divorce—the highest rate in the world.[3] Although divorce and separation are the main causes of single parenthood, out-of-wedlock childbearing is a second factor. In 1960, only 5 percent of all live births in the United States were to unmarried women. By 1988, more than 25 percent of U.S. births were to unwed mothers, often adolescents.[4] In most metropolitan areas, the number is much higher. To make matters even more difficult, single parenthood and poverty often go hand-in-hand. Forty-three percent of mothers-only families are poor, compared to only 7 percent of two-parent families.[5]

For families of all kinds, one of the most dramatic changes of the past two decades has been the increase in the number of mothers working outside the home. Between 1970 and 1990, the proportion of mothers with children under age six working or looking for work outside the home rose from 32 percent to 58 percent.[6] By 1990, 74 percent of women with children between the ages of six and thirteen were working or looking for work.[7] Fewer than 10 percent of the nation's children live in traditional families with stay-at-home mothers, working fathers, and one or more children.

A Legacy of Doubts, A Legacy of Choices

CATHY. ©1986 by Cathy Guisewite. Reprinted with permission of UNIVERSAL PRESS SYNDICATE. All rights reserved.

These changes have often had radical implications for family life. Judy Mann, writing for *The Washington Post*, observed that what parents are left with today is "a legacy of doubts, a legacy of choices."[8] Lifestyles, like silverware patterns, household products, and clothing designs, are influenced not only by economics but also by historical and political events, the media, and popular trends. In the wake of the women's movement and for the generation who came of professional age in the 1970s and 1980s, having it all was supposed to include a house in the suburbs, a rewarding career, a successful marriage, children, daycare, and household help. This vision is now being challenged by a new generation of parents who do not readily identify with the activism, anger, or self-absorption often expressed in past decades. What many parents now recognize is that there are always trade-offs in life; that for everything gained, something is lost; that decisions made by parents have consequences on the family. Research on the family is beginning to suggest that parental presence is important, that children who spend their early years with mom or dad are less vulnerable to problems throughout childhood and into their adult lives.[9] Children need the continuity of a love that is provided by someone who is committed to their welfare without reservation.[10] Ultimately, what may be best for some adults is not always best for their children and families or for a society dependent upon strong families.

Divorce

Rabbi Harold Kushner, author of *When Bad Things Happen to Good People* and *When All You've Ever Wanted Isn't Enough*, acknowledges that although many parents are emotionally able to survive a divorce—perhaps even emerging from the experience as stronger, more independent people—children are far more vulnerable. Kushner wonders if

We may be raising a generation of young people who will grow up afraid to love, afraid to give themselves completely to another person, because they will have seen how much it hurts to take the risk of loving and having it not work out. They will be looking for intimacy without risk, pleasure without significant emotional involvement. They will be so fearful of the pain and disappointment that they will forego the possibilities of love and joy.[11]

Divorce, according to marriage counselor and author O. Dean Martin, is the solution to only one problem—an unworkable marriage. Increasingly, however, couples are breaking up due to extraneous circumstances such as the inability to cope with job and schedule stresses, midlife crises, a reluctance to grow up, or the relentless pressures of subliminal stimuli[12] which constantly and subtly shape their expectations and views of themselves and their lives, marriages, and families.

Marriage and Family Life

Marriages have difficulty thriving when couples do not have enough time for each other. With increased frequency, marriage counselors are seeing professional couples who cannot cope with the stress of two jobs, family responsibilities, and community obligations. Men as well as women are experiencing stress because of escalating expectations. Fatigue robs couples of energy, passion, and follow-through. Those few hours a day devoted to family somehow just don't seem to add up to quality time. One current researcher has found that parents spend 40 percent less time with their children than they did fifteen years ago.[13] It is easy to be overwhelmed with maintaining a house or making a living to the detriment of building a home. The urgency of such chores as grocery shopping, laundry, at-home job assignments, car pooling, and house cleaning frequently preempts the more important activities of talking, caring, listening, experiencing, and learning together. For single parents who shoulder all the responsibilities themselves, the challenge is even more awesome.

Daycare

The flip side of parents spending less time with their children is that children are spending more time being influenced by individuals outside the family. This is especially true with daycare.

Learning to balance the demands of career and family is a constant challenge to conscientious parents. Daycare decisions are especially difficult, even for parents whose financial circumstances can assure high-quality care. For many parents whose financial resources are slim the problem may seem insurmountable at times. Unlicensed daycare or overburdened babysitters can hardly be depended upon to address the nurturing and learning needs of children. Other situations raise concerns about the physical safety of children as many parents, especially of older children, are allowing children to babysit themselves for a time each day. We recall a child in our neighborhood who, beginning in kindergarten, came home each day to fumble for a key left under the doormat, fix her own lunch, and await the evening return of her mother. The mother expressed pride in her daughter's maturity. Increasingly, however, those who work with children emphasize that worldly sophistication isn't the same thing as maturity at all. Although a child may learn how to operate the microwave, VCR, and PC, what he or she may miss are lessons in loving, trusting, sacrificing, and sharing. Without a solid foundation in these social skills and values, a child is often incapable of passing them on to his or her own children.

Television and Videos

Children left alone for long periods of time often turn to TV to help structure their time. It is easy to understand why many parents prefer that their children watch TV to alternative ways of spending time which might require safety concerns. For all children, TV has become the most powerful of teachers. Not only do children learn their numbers and letters by watching TV, but they observe and pick up lessons on values that even the program producers don't always intend. Can all problems be solved in a half-hour with two commercial breaks? Will breath mints make a person popular or sexy? Do all football players drink? The implications are endless. Who monitors these messages?

Add to TV the values implied in many movies and some youth music. Add perennial peer pressure and our culture's insistent claim that material possessions are the source of success, status, and happiness. Parents, even if they are committed to teaching their children alternative values, seem to be at a considerable disadvantage. According to columnist Ellen Goodman, there has been a "fundamental shift," and parents who were "once expected to rear children in accordance with dominant cultural messages so often today need "to raise their children in opposition."[14] Content aside, our children's viewing habits (as well as those of many adults) are causing them to become increasingly sedentary spectators, dependent upon others for entertainment, stimulation, and time structuring.

Presence, Not Presents

Many parents have simply given up. They reluctantly resign themselves to a loss of control over their children's lives, and when they lose that control, they also lose the ability to protect their children. Children are exposed at earlier and earlier ages to realities with which they have neither the maturity nor the guidance to cope. They are being forced to grow up too fast in terms of exposure and experience. In many cases, the X-rated videos that are all-too-available to younger viewers only fill in the details of the complex dating relationships they observe daily in the lives of their own divorced parents.

Many parents, perhaps to compensate for the time they cannot seem to give their children, are especially vulnerable to pressure to buy things, not recognizing how much more important their presence is than their presents are. Children today seem driven not only by the desire to own things but also the compulsion to own the right things. What often matters is the correct label, the right model, or the popular series—attributes which frequently apply for only one season at a time. From designer diapers to sports cars, many children are denied nothing except what they need most—the dependability of an active, present, caring family. "My working has enabled us to buy extra things for our kids," wrote one mother, "and that used to alleviate some of my guilt feelings about not spending more time with them, but, to my horror, it is clear that the kids now prefer having the 'things' over spending time with me."[15]

We have a friend who teaches sixth grade in an affluent suburban neighborhood outside Washington, D.C. Her students represent a range of backgrounds, and our friend, along with her teaching teammate, has established a remarkable rapport with her students. Some of these young people, not seduced by the purchases of their parents, had the insight, despite the pain, to share their feelings upon returning to school after a holiday. A written assignment inspired the following responses:

> "I got seven computer games for Christmas, but what I really wanted was to see my dad."

> "My brother and I went to six movies over the holidays, but I wish my family could have spent it together again."

The world may have changed, but the needs of children have not. They still need the love, understanding, acceptance, accountability, control, and protection of the family.

CHOICES

If the post-Superparent era has left Americans with a legacy of doubts, the encouraging news is that it has also left them a legacy of choices. Women are secure enough in the workforce that they can talk openly about the difficulties of combining home and career. Many women today establish a career first and then begin a family—hence the increase of first-time parents over thirty years old. The choice to suspend, delay, or interrupt a career to have children is causing fewer raised eyebrows than it did only a few years ago. Both women and men are discovering that personal worth is defined not only in terms of career achievement, just as women earlier discovered that personal worth is defined not only in terms of family roles.

What is largely discounted in to-work-or-not-to-work discussions is the fact that, for many women, a choice does not even exist. Many women, like men, work because they must work in order to support their families. The legacy of choices is compromised when society provides little support for those choices. Shared positions and part-time careers, for example, are options to which more lip service than implementation has been given. There is still a critical need for affordable, high-quality preschool and daycare programs. Only recently have many communities begun to experiment with special programs for latchkey kids, not only teaching them household skills but also offering hotlines and after-school activities. Perhaps family advocates in the future would do well to focus their attention on encouraging private and public programs which help support the range of decisions parents will be making—whether by helping women return to work after years as full-time homemakers or by supporting the daycare needs of dual-career couples. Whatever models emerge must be sensitive to the need for both men and women to contribute to the support of families without compromising the future of children.

If parents think of their lives as books, then there must be some chapters in which children are the key characters. The plot has to revolve around the actions, activities, and development of the children. Homes have to be settings for the interests and involvements parents and children share. The theme of these chapters must be to guide children in such a way that they grow into self-responsible adults. There are many chapters in a parent's life, but none are more important than those in which children appear.

FAMILY STRENGTHS LITERATURE

In the past, much research on families has been problem-oriented (i.e., what's wrong with families), and studies that focus on concerns such as abuse, divorce, alcoholism, or adolescent pregnancy are valuable in helping society frame solutions to these problems. Family strengths research, on the other hand, is a relatively new field that focuses not on what's *wrong* with families but on what's *right* and how strength can be discovered, duplicated, and developed. In the spring of 1990, the U.S. Department of Health and Human Services convened a conference of family strengths researchers in Washington, D.C. One outcome of that meeting was a document[16] that summarized the family strengths literature to date and included a consensus list of factors which research indicates contributes to family strength. Conference participants reached an agreement that the following constructs were "the basic dimensions of strong, healthy families":[17]

Communication

Encouragement of individuals

Expressing appreciation

Commitment to family

Religious/spiritual orientation

Social connectedness

Ability to adapt

Clear roles

Time together[18]

Such a list represents a scientific way of saying that home and family are important. At the deepest level, home and family help define human beings.

HOME A HAVEN

For most people, the word *home* conjures up images of a place where one is welcomed with genuine affection and loved without reservation, a place to belong. To come home is to find this safe harbor, a refuge from a world which changes rapidly and demands much. It suggests a place to relax and be renewed without the relentless pressure to be productive or profound.

Not only movies, music, the media, literature, and the arts, but indeed, human tradition itself holds up the idea of home as a safe haven. Those whose personal experiences least resemble this ideal image are probably most compelled by the possibilities. They often spend their lives mourning what they've missed and missing opportunities to create what they desire. Regardless of what home actually means, most know almost intuitively what home should mean—first and foremost, a place where one is loved and accepted.

Adults need to keep in touch with the havens in their lives, whether those havens take the form of favorite places, special relationships, or intellectual and spiritual pursuits. These havens present opportunities for restoration, renewal, and growth, and they can serve as tune-ups or turning points in one's human journey. When the emotional needs of adults are met, they become free to concentrate their talents and energies on different pursuits. This liberation from self-absorption enables adults to be more attentive to the needs of others. For the giving and the receiving to grow out of the loving and being loved is to characterize family relationships at their best.

For children, however, the experience of home as a haven is more than just a helpful head start in life. It is one of the most important human needs and, left unfulfilled, it can educationally handicap or emotionally cripple a person for life. This need to belong is so universal that, in our better moments, we can glimpse a vision of a world in which all humans belong to one family.

HOMEWORK

But home is not only a place to experience love and acceptance; it is also where human beings learn and grow. It is not only a haven but also a school, and parents are the first teachers. Parents are, after all, society's primary information givers, although the information they pass on isn't always data. At home children learn the first and, for many, most important lessons of their lives, from both the words they hear and the actions they see. When education in the family is adequate, it prepares children for the world outside the home as well as that within. They learn to give and receive affection. They learn how to have fun and how to handle defeat. They learn to express enthusiasm, sorrow, anger, and concern. They learn to laugh, cry, and relate to others. They learn values that will guide their decisions throughout life. They learn self-discipline, accountability, and skills for living, coping, and organizing. They learn to think and care about others. The family is a primary support group, helping its members acquire the habits and attitudes they need and providing opportunity for practice in a protected environment, consolation for failure, and encouragement to try again.

Children's needs for both acceptance and accountability are a dual responsibility for parents. Generations as well as individuals have sometimes seen these needs as mutually exclusive and discounted the significance of one or the other in their parenting. Some adults today recall having grown up in homes where a parent never actually said 'I love you' or expressed affection in tangible terms. Probably more common today are parents who, as a consequence of busy schedules, discount complementary emotional needs for structure, instruction, and discipline. When responsibility and accountability are missing in parenting, children become conditioned to believe that their wishes, needs, and desires take precedence over those of others. Such self-centeredness is a set-up for frustration, alienation, and loneliness. Children need the security of limits, the protection of parental restraint, and the opportunity to learn self-discipline in the home just as they need acceptance and love.

Some years ago, there was much discussion in theological circles about a concept called "cheap grace," and different theologians found themselves favoring one emphasis or another, either the miracle of unconditional acceptance or the challenge of uncompromising expectations. In the family, there is the same tension. It is the teaching which complements and strengthens the acceptance. It is the acceptance which gives credibility to the teaching.

2

Cohesion:
What Families Share

The word *cohesion* is used to describe a tendency to stick together. In high school physics classes, *cohesion* is defined as the force that holds the molecules of a substance together, often resulting in the creation of a whole that is stronger than the simple sum of its parts. It may be the universe's version of Super Glue.

What is it, then, that causes *families* to stick together? Are there any forces or factors that are cohesive for families? What draws families closer and helps them create an identity above and beyond the mere sum of their membership? Is there a Super Glue for families?

We believe that what helps hold families together is what they share in common. Family cohesion is reinforced through all those actions, beliefs, and attitudes that help characterize the family as a unit and thus become part of the family's self-definition. Shared activities, traditions, conversations, commitment, and—most significantly—values provide the content of a family's identity and helps it to understand what it means to be a Johnson, a Lucas, or an Asaka! The key to cohesiveness is what is shared in common. To consciously strengthen these factors is to strengthen families.

STRONG FAMILIES SHARE TIME AND EXPERIENCES

Close relationships take time and grow out of a foundation of shared experiences. Families do things together because they enjoy being together, and they enjoy being together because of all they do together. The range of shared activities varies with a particular family's age, stage, and interests—from at-home activities such as reading, talking, and playing games to outdoor activities such as sports or camping trips. We know one family who skis in the winter and sails in the summer. Another enjoys competitive highland dancing and Scottish bagpiping, with various family members participating as judge, teacher, or participant. Some families seem to move through the seasons with sports—from football to basketball to baseball, from Little League participation to professional sports viewing. Others structure their shared times around extended family get-togethers or church activities. For both of us, some of our treasured childhood memories are of family get-togethers with parents, grandparents, sisters, brothers, aunts, uncles, and cousins gathered together to talk, eat, laugh, and share. Recently we saw a mother and daughter who had commemorated similar experiences in their family with matching T-shirts picturing a large, leafy tree and the words "We Are Family," the family name, and the date of their last reunion.

PLAN TO PLAY

Taking time to do things together is important. Yet, if there is any refrain commonly echoed by parents today, it is that they just don't have enough time for family activities. That old quality-versus-quantity cliché that was supposed to bring comfort instead of guilt has little meaning when parents are consistently exhausted, both physically and emotionally. For many families, stress has become routine, a long-term lifestyle instead of a temporary problem. But children are more than just another activity in a busy schedule. They both complicate and enrich our lives. At a minimum, the key to more family time is planning and prioritizing. Once parents decide that time together as a family is important, their planning must permit it. Even opportunities for spontaneity must often be planned. We know single working parents who are more successful at finding family time than two-parent families with stay-at-home parents. These parents have learned to use the calendar to schedule opportunities for closeness. They structure time together into their lives, whether as regular at-home nights or as outings, trips, and family activities. In addition, they set aside time for unstructured activities, evenings just to stay at home or Saturdays with nothing planned. In our own family, we became aware of the importance of both activity and inactivity when our daughter wrote in a sixth-grade autobiography, "I look forward to an eventful and unstructured future." The key is balance, an unreachable goal for those who do not plan at all. There will always be demands on parents' time that compete with family activities. What's important must be part of the regular schedule.

Sometimes families need to review their commitments in order to free up more family time. Some parents discover that almost all of their discretionary time is spent car-pooling or supporting a range of children's activities from football to soccer to cheerleading to music lessons to dancing. Which activities are really important to the child? Which ones do the family as a whole enjoy? How many group activities does each child need? Is the child becoming dependent upon others for structuring his or her time? Can any of the children's activities take place while the parents are working to save after-work time for family activities? These are questions each family must address individually.

Parents, too, can get caught in the trap of over-involvement to the detriment of the family, even when engaged in a host of worthwhile activities such as PTA, church work, and community service. Priority setting is in order for parents at home as well as at work. How can parents balance the need to be present for their families with their responsibilities to schools, communities, churches, and synagogues—organizations that depend on volunteer assistance? A major commitment in one area may preclude a commitment in another. The year that one serves as church lay leader may have to be the year one contents oneself with merely attending PTA meetings. A parent who is an officer in the PTA may have to decline an office in a community group. Many parents find themselves so over-committed that they readily identify with cartoon character Sally Forth when she decides to take time to relax only to have her husband remind her that they must be at a PTA meeting in fifteen minutes.[1]

SOMETHING FOR EVERYONE

Some schools and churches, sensitive to the competition for parents' time, are beginning to structure more activities with something for everyone. One community's middle school sponsors activities for the children concurrently with programs for parents. Churches frequently plan intergenerational programs. Such activities help counter a strong tendency in our society to segregate people by age.

To make time in their lives for family, parents must be more intentional about the use of time, especially discretionary time. They may well find that other areas of their lives suffer from a lack of focused attention. Spring cleaning or home repair projects could very well evolve into year-long ventures, or a parent might have to take longer to finish a degree. It may take parents longer to reach some goals, but one does not measure a happy home in the same way as one measures high positions, degrees after one's name, or social status.

The time families spend together and the activities they share help build family cohesion, especially when those bonds are built early in a family's life. Being together then becomes a need that all family members experience, as well as a way of having fun. Family members come to depend on their time together as a source of individual satisfaction and family identity. We are amazed at how many young people continue to value participation in family activities as they grow older. This seems to be particularly true in homes where there has not only been a firm foundation of shared activities but also a respect for each individual's interests and, especially, a respect for adolescents' needs for space and distance. As children grow into young adults, family time becomes an opportunity and an invitation, not a burden or compulsion. Most adolescents can accept the necessity of subordinating their individual schedules to an occasional family activity that is especially important to the parents. Mutual respect, consideration, and compromise are the skills a young person needs to make the transition from complete parental control of the schedule to the adolescent becoming responsible for her time, commitments, and schedule.

Also important is parental willingness to expand interests, if not participation, to fit those of growing adolescents. We recall our children's enthusiasm about skiing in the aftermath of a trip with the church youth group. Eager for us to share the fun, they talked us into going along the next time. To say that skiing is not my sport of choice is putting it mildly. And spending the entire day on the bunny slope was not my only claim to fame. I also had the distinction of being the only person to fall off the chair lift! Our children still enjoy skiing a couple times each year, but now we watch them over hot chocolate from the ski resort snack bar.

Ski trips and picnics, sports and games, music and art, reading and working, even just watching TV together—these are but a few examples of opportunities for families to share good times and build needed closeness.

STRONG FAMILIES SHARE RITUALS AND TRADITIONS

Some experiences are especially potent, not only because they are shared, but because they are also predictable and repeated. Rituals and traditions are familiar events that help pull families together. Passed along from one generation to the next, traditions establish continuity with the past and identity with the present extended family. We once heard the transition from one generation to the next compared to the passing of the baton by runners in a relay race. In recent years, it seems, the baton is often dropped as families, displaced from their origins, neglect to repeat past rituals or create new ones. The assurance of belonging and mutual dependency have too often been replaced by loneliness and isolation. A friend recently told us about a Jewish temple that incorporated into its bar mitzvah ceremonies a ritual symbolizing the importance of passing the torch on to the next generation. When the Torah is removed from the ark, the grandfather gives it to the father, who then passes it on to his son. The Torah becomes a symbol of the son's accepting responsibility for carrying his religious faith into the next generation.

In today's volatile, changing world, traditions are more important than ever before. People have little control over much of what affects their lives, and today's solutions often seem to address yesterday's problems. Individuals can't even anticipate what anxieties might lie ahead. What people are expected to know is sometimes overwhelming; how they are comfortable responding is often obsolete. Traditions can give a sense of connection by helping to anchor one securely in the present while building a bridge between the past and the future. Rituals can help one celebrate, grieve, reconcile, and grow. Many American Indian cultures have rich legacies of ritualized behavior, often expressed through ceremony and custom, to help individuals along in their life journeys and to pass on tribal values. Families can also use rituals to strengthen and support their traditions.

Anthropologist Brett Williams believes that traditions are crucial to family health. "You've got to make some things special," he advises. "Imagine a family where nothing was very special— not meals, not bath time, not holidays, not birthdays. Eventually, the children get the message that they're not important, that life doesn't mean much."[2]

Building Bridges

Alex Haley's book, *Roots*, which chronicles several generations of an African-American family, renewed interest in genealogy in the United States. People searched out their family roots and discovered in the process that, for families and individuals as well as for historians, the past is important to the present. There are lessons in history for all. People may belong to the present, but they will always be indebted to the past and responsible for the future. How can parents help build these important bridges for their children? For families who live close to grandparents and other relatives, the opportunities for bridge-building are readily available through family get-togethers. Such gatherings are equally valued by the younger generation and by their parents, grandparents, aunts, and uncles—all of whom not only love one another but also share values, perspective, and experiences. The circle of those who can provide models for and who care about each child expands, with an increased awareness of accountability by each person.

Because of distance, illness, or other reasons, many families are not able to be in regular touch with relatives. Where geography separates families, letters, tapes, and phone calls can help diminish the distance. Pictures, slides, or stories, acted out with the aid of paper dolls, may help very small children visualize grandparents and other relatives who love them very much even though they live far away. Greeting cards or small gifts sent on special occasions often serve as reminders of those who care but can't be there.

Children who have lost grandparents or other relatives through death can still be helped to feel a sense of continuity as parents share impressions of their growing-up years and past loved ones. Tangible reminders such as photographs help children relate to their roots. Gary's mother has made quilts for each of her children, with Gary's consisting of materials taken from dresses and shirts worn by his grandparents. This heirloom, passed on to future generations, will help tell the family's story.

When specific extended family situations present few opportunities for intergenerational sharing, parents need to seek such relationships elsewhere. Some churches and social service organizations sponsor foster grandparent programs or other special activities that help bring generations together in loving, caring, and supportive ways. When a young mother from our church died, leaving a husband and six-year-old daughter, church members brought together their memories, impressions, and photographs of this woman in a special scrapbook to be given to her daughter later.

TELLING THE STORY

Rituals and traditions are more than just events at holiday times. Family traditions also include stories, songs, customs, and expressions. When one of our children came home from elementary school complaining that a classmate had accused him of wearing 'high waters,' (too-short pants), I suddenly remembered the way my mother described the same phenomenon: "You look like Charley Pontius." When I asked her to explain the family expression, she traced it back to her mother and Osceola, Indiana, where a chubby, friendly fellow who ran the local grocery store always wore his trousers a bit short. Two generations later and our kids looked 'like Charley Pontius.' Another of my grandmother's favorite expressions, which she used to describe a child in need of a haircut, was: "You look like Strickland's dog." I never saw Strickland's dog, but I know when one of our sons begins to look like 'Strickland's dog.'

My grandfather, who died when I was twelve years old, would sometimes sing to us when we went to visit. I particularly remember one song that told the story of a man who climbed a persimmon tree to escape a pursuing bear. The mournful refrain went: "Oh, Lord, if you can't help me, please don't help the bear." Years later, when our children were little, I replayed a part of my past when I heard my father sing that same song to our children. Examples like these—legends, stories, songs, expressions, habits, talents, and values from the past—comprise a family fabric for each of us, a colorful quilt of real-life experiences which each family passes on to the next generation.

RITUAL BY RESOLUTION

What about families where the generational baton has been dropped, where family flashbacks produce few scenes to be remembered, traditions to be repeated, or rituals to be shared? These families (as well as others who simply wish to enrich the legacy they've been given) need not regret. Rituals and traditions can be the result of resolution as well as evolution. Opportunities for new traditions are limited only by one's imagination. Births, trips, recipes, birthdays, coming-of-age observances, holidays, weddings, showers, anniversaries, the first day of school, the transition to college, the day the braces come off—the list is endless. These are the raw materials of family life. When our daughter got her driver's license, we surprised her with a cake. With two younger brothers watching, we knew we had started a tradition that ultimately included the cake, a greeting card, and a key chain as the necessary props. When another of the children, then a preschooler, requested fondue for birthday dinner, we had no way of knowing that fondue would become standard birthday fare three times a year at our house.

Finally, families must remember that flexibility and openness are necessary if traditions are going to work positively. As new families form, the families of origin must allow for adaptations of customs and traditions. For example, the new family can't celebrate Christmas Eve with both sets of relatives, even if this is the traditional time in each case. When we were married, one side of the family decided to hold its Christmas celebration on New Year's Day, giving us the opportunity to spend Christmas Day at home with our children. Over the years, we have developed a host of special Christmas traditions of our own, without having to miss the celebration with the larger family.

Rituals are not meant to be burdens or invoke guilt. They are designed to bring families continuity, warmth, and joy. As families keep this in mind, they can repeat, evolve, resolve and create their own sets of traditions. Some traditions can be repeated from the past with almost no change, whereas others may need to be recycled to fit today's tastes and lifestyles. Some may be discarded, others invented. In this way, rituals can be used to strengthen families, not abused by turning them into straitjackets.

Adolescents will especially appreciate their parents' flexibility in accommodating complicated schedules to allow them to be part of family experiences they don't want to miss. We can recall times when a birthday celebration was changed to another date or an Advent ceremony was held on a day other than Sunday. All families make their own adjustments and accommodations and, in the process, decide who they are and what is important to them.

Rituals and traditions are among the best memory-makers in family life. Dostoyesvky understood the importance of people growing up with positive memories of childhood. In the concluding paragraphs of *The Brothers Karamazov*, he wrote:

> *My dear children, perhaps you won't understand what I am saying to you . . . but you will remember it all the same, and will agree with my words sometime. You must know that there is nothing higher and stronger and more wholesome and good for life in the future than some good memory, especially a memory of childhood, of home. People talk to you a good deal about your education, but some good, sacred memory, preserved from childhood, is, perhaps, the best education. If a man [or woman] carries many such memories with him into life, he is safe to the end of his days, and if one has only one good memory left in one's heart, even that may sometimes be the means of saving us.*[3]

The memories we pass on to future generations may save more than our families.

Strong Families Share the Details of Their Daily Lives

There is universal agreement on the importance of communication in all relationships, family ones included. Any time books, articles, commentaries, or conversations address relationships, they inevitably turn to the subject of communication. Communication is frequently cited as a reason for success or maligned as an explanation for failure. Parents are challenged to talk with their children so that the children will talk with them. Disagreements at work are frequently described as 'breakdowns in communication.' Even allowing for the hyperbole of the popular press, it is difficult to overstate the importance of communication in successful family functioning. This comes as no surprise to most. It is almost as if people are conditioned to respond in litany fashion to the familiar questions with their equally predictable answers:

What is the biggest problem in relationships today? *Communication.*

What do parents need to learn to do to cope better with their children? *Communicate.*

What causes the most problems at work? *Communication.*

Why did they break up? *They couldn't communicate.*

When our children were little, we got a book about icebergs from the local library. Among the fascinating findings in this book was the fact that only ten percent of an iceberg appears above the surface of the water. There is much more to an iceberg than one sees. Communication is similar: there is more there than meets the eye. Communication includes talking and listening, confronting and praising, commanding and comforting, approving and disapproving, reinforcing, discounting, and modeling. It is verbal and nonverbal, positive and negative. It is an attitude, an action, a smile, a frown, a hug, a handshake, a kick, a kiss, a tone of voice, a facial expression. We can communicate with words, sounds, looks, or gestures. We can communicate through art, poetry, music, and dance. To communicate, one shares not only facts and information but also values and beliefs, hopes and dreams, memories and feelings.

Put simply, communication is any way in which people exchange meaning with others. It helps define humanness. To understand communication in this broad perspective, one can see at once why there is so much agreement about its importance to family relationships.

Good communication is the means by which families express affection, teach control, build cohesiveness, and initiate relationships. It is the tie that binds all other family strengths. Rather than view communication in isolation, we have tried to weave it throughout and show how certain attitudes, actions, insights, and skills help families exchange meaning in ways that strengthen and support.

If someone were to ask us what the most significant indicator of good communication in a family is, we would not point to how the family handles conflict, as important as that is. We would not check out their skills in assertiveness or problem-solving. Whether they were well-versed in the latest child-rearing techniques would be of little importance to us. We would not even count the times the family used praise, as valuable as that is. We believe that the hallmark of good communication is the way in which family members express interest in each other's lives. A genuine interest in each other, reflected in everyday family conversations, is one factor that builds cohesiveness and emphasizes that we are all important to each other. What children need most today is someone who is totally committed to their welfare.

Sharing with each other freely and listening to each other with interest are the foundations of family communication. In good families, members can share not only important events and profound thoughts, but also the mundane, the trivial, and the insignificant. In such families, people can repeat the recognition they have received without embarrassment and confess their failures without fearing loss of esteem.

The importance of these everyday communications was brought home to us the year our daughter started college. Lisa was especially homesick the first month or so and wrote that the problem with college was that: "No one is interested in the details of your daily life." She went on to elaborate: "I would say to my roommate, 'Well, I'm going downstairs to get some ice,' and she would give me this that's-nice-Lisa-but-why-are-you-telling-me look." Families need to be interested in the details of each others lives.

The confidence and trust that this interest is present begins early in life. From almost the moment of birth, a child will attempt to respond and communicate. Babies, even in the first weeks of life, observe and mimic nonverbal communication. Soon they reproduce the sounds needed for language development. As family members encourage and participate in this conversation, babies learn that they are important, part of the family, and worthy of attention. They begin to develop a strong ego—an important task of their growing-up years. When parents fail to respond to a child's early attempts to communicate, the physical and psychological damage can be devastating. T. Berry Brazelton, sometimes called 'the working parent's Dr. Spock,' recorded the reactions of small babies when their mothers failed to respond to their conversations. Even a three-month old child will quickly turn inward when its mother does not respond. Such a dramatic demonstration is designed to help *all* parents keep their priorities in order. If parents are too busy to talk to their children, then they are too busy.

Obviously, parents have other relationships and concerns and cannot be equally interested in and responsive to their children at all times. That is neither a realistic nor an ultimately beneficial goal. Children, however, need to be able to rely on their parents' interest and attention on a regular basis. All too often, parents miss the best opportunities. Riding on a commuter train one day, we noticed two young mothers with toddlers in tow. Neither responded to her child's questions or comments. Neither heard because each was 'plugged in' via headphones to a local radio station.

In many households, frequent conversations and the opportunities for closeness they bring have gone the way of other time spent together. Such moments are sacrificed to busy schedules; rushing has become the norm. Even during those rare moments when families *are* together, TV viewing often limits talking time to commercials and station breaks.

TABLE TALK

In some families, talking times may need to be structured into the day. Although good times will vary according to family schedules and the ages of children, for many families the most logical choice is mealtime. Noting that we have to eat anyway, author Letty Cottin Pogrebin suggests that mealtimes can be a "great opportunity for intimacy and influence if we but take the trouble to establish the tradition of talk and other closeness rituals."[4] Some parents are so protective of this time together that they take the phone off the hook until the meal is over. Others delay dinnertime to accommodate sports practices, for example; still others may save dessert for everybody to share later. The point is that, unless an extraordinary effort is made to preserve it, in many homes the occasion of the family meal will disappear and the house will become a restaurant/motel where people come and go on different schedules, satisfying appetites with microwave meals and meeting each other only in passing.

Making the most of mealtimes may require that parents suspend their preoccupation with making points—such as teaching table manners—which can be detrimental to family conversations. A child's eating Jello with his fingers may be too much for his parents, but it is all too easy for parents to turn mealtimes into corrective sessions which aid neither good digestion nor family closeness. A private, after-dinner lesson with the needful child on how to hold a fork may pay off in better manners as well as a better relationship than a reprimand in front of everybody.

Our family sometimes uses mealtime to play trivia games, tell jokes and stories, or update each other on the day's activities. As the children have grown older, they are often eager to raise the trivia question that is sure to stump Mom and Dad (not a difficult task). Young people may enjoy philosophical, political, or religious conversations that provide them opportunities to try out new ideas on their parents.

SHARING WITH HUMOR

Humor is another effective way of building conversational closeness in families. It is fascinating to observe the growth of a child's sense of humor from the ask-me-if-I'm-a-Cheerio stage to the adolescent's sophisticated appreciation of puns. When parents are a responsive audience, children are eager to share the latest jokes. In this way, parents not only build rapport in the family, but they also nurture in children something of inestimable value—a sense of humor.

Sharing the details of daily life is not a panacea in family communication. It deals, after all, with only a part of what communication is all about. But it is a giant step forward in building the reliability, security, and trust upon which all communication rests. When parents set aside time for talking, they affirm the importance of each person as an individual and the family as a unit. These talking times help keep families close.

STRONG FAMILIES SHARE A COMMITMENT TO THE FAMILY

Was the 'do your own thing' of the 'me-generation' just a passing fad, or did it leave a lasting imprint on family life in the United States? Were self-awareness, self-achievement, self-assertion, and self-indulgence emphasized at the expense of shared relationships? Has our country sacrificed family stability for individual achievement and recognition? Is it possible that the quest for personal happiness has not only proved elusive but often reaped its opposite? Many second thoughts have grown out of the social upheaval and role redefinitions of the past few decades. Some see such factors as the high divorce rate, the rise in family abuse statistics, alcohol and drug difficulties, and street violence as direct outcomes of the 'me first' mentality. Many parents today recognize that decisions have consequences on the family and that what is best for the parents as individuals may not necessarily be what is best for the children or the family. Behind the individual success stories there are always trade-offs, and families must be aware of what they are giving up as well as what they are gaining. There will always be choices. Fathers and mothers alike are increasingly beginning to weigh the price as well as the prize of certain career decisions. A successful sales manager whose job required frequent trips away from his family pondered the hours he had spent waiting in offices and airport lobbies "thinking how lucky you are to be an executive and living this glamorous life. It's exhausting and it shrinks your soul."[5]

For parents to consider family factors in decision-making may mean that a couple decides to weather a stormy time in their marriage rather than to split. It may mean that some parents decide to turn down promotions that require relocation because of the disruption to the family. We know of one successful company that opted not to expand when none of its key employees wanted to move to another part of the country to manage a new plant. Some companies, recognizing that successful family relationships can help a person be more productive on the job, have responded with sensitivity to family needs by permitting job sharing, part-time work, or flexible hours for parents of small children. Other companies have organized on-site daycare. Many parents negotiate their own compromises by taking turns staying home, with a sick child, for example. In other homes, either the father or the mother becomes the primary caregiver to the children while the other functions as the primary wage earner. Or one parent may work part-time or work at home.

Realistically, such innovative options are easier to suggest than to apply. In making choices, families must consider future payoffs as well as short-term benefits, and economics frequently limits the options available to them. Careers are important, not only to individuals but to families and the nation as well. A change of address, for example, doesn't always have negative consequences on the family. A child dead set against a move may find the new situation to his or her liking and the parents may find it supportive of the family unit. All decisions have risks. The point is that when it comes to the decisions parents make, the impact on the family must be considered. The assurance that the family as a unit is important inspires individual commitment and helps keep families together. Strong families know that it means something to be a family.

STRONG FAMILIES SHARE VALUES

PINOCCHIO: *Am I a real boy?*

BLUE FAIRY: *No, Pinocchio—to make Geppetto's wish come true will be entirely up to you.*

PINOCCHIO: *Up to me?*

BLUE FAIRY: *Prove yourself brave, truthful and unselfish, and someday you will be a real boy.*

PINOCCHIO: *A real boy!*

BLUE FAIRY: *You must learn to choose between right and wrong.*

PINOCCHIO: *Right and wrong? But how will I know?*

BLUE FAIRY: *Your conscience will tell you.*[6]

The story of *Pinocchio* is about the perennial struggle between good and evil as the wooden marionette learns what happens to those who resist the straight and narrow way. In the end, Pinocchio becomes a real boy because he is brave, truthful, and unselfish. He learns to let his conscience be his guide.

Of course, the presupposition behind the story is that Pinocchio had a conscience and that certain actions such as deceit and disobedience were wrong. From a contemporary perspective, Pinocchio's world may seem enviously uncomplicated. The choices, if not always easy, were at least clear. Not only is the world in which real boys and girls live today more complex but the consciences they consult are also more ambiguous.

Instead of supplying children with workable values and helpful guidelines to enable them to cope with the complexities of
the modern world, many parents today communicate just the
opposite. When they consult their consciences, young people often discover that the confusion within is greater than the confusion without. Because of a lack of confidence or simply a lack of
time, parents frequently blur right and wrong and good and bad
in their teaching.

There are, according to newspaper columnist William Raspberry, "built-in limits" that have historically governed the behavior of most people and thus seem almost natural. These include prohibitions against certain things that most people
would never do, such as "snatch[ing] a watch off an old lady's
arm or inflict[ing] gratuitous pain on another human being, or
deliberately ruin[ing] a lovely work of art."[7] Likewise, there are
certain positive actions, such as "keep[ing] our commitments,
pay[ing] our bills, give[ing] a honest day's work for our wages,
and return[ing] found wallets." What frightens Raspberry and
others is the increasing number of individuals, "especially young
people, who seem almost devoid of such controls." The nation's
capital was stunned by the story of two twelve-year-old boys
who pushed a seven-year-old into a creek and threw stones at
him until he drowned so that they could steal his bicycle. "What
saddens me," confessed a friend of ours who teaches sixth
grade, "is that I know children who could do such a thing. I've
had them in class."

Increasingly it is teachers, who often spend more time with
children than their parents do, who appreciate the urgency of
the need to teach values. In a national poll of 1,346 teachers
conducted by the Education Research Service,[8] 92 percent
maintained that teaching ethical character was a major objective in education, and 95 percent thought teaching citizenship
was also.

Unfortunately, some have confused the ethics issue with the
campaign to reinstate school prayer. There is a difference between supporting state-sanctioned religion in the schools and
advocating moral instruction in the curriculum. Children do not
develop character by osmosis; they must be taught. To strive for
values-neutral instruction is to misunderstand that the survival
of any society is dependent upon widely shared values, even if

respect for diversity is one of those values. There should not, therefore, be any debate in our schools about the rightness or wrongness of actions such as lying, stealing, or cheating, and yet these behaviors are commonplace in many schools. In a recent survey at one high school, 90 percent of the students said they saw nothing wrong with cheating.

The educational community has responded to these concerns with organizations such as the American Institute for Character Education, with values-sensitive materials, and with recommendations for teachers and schools such as those issued in the 1980s as part of a report popularly called 'The Thanksgiving Statement.'[9] Signed by twenty-seven public officials, university professors, and public administrators, this report (officially called "Developing Character — Transmitting Knowledge") recommends that, among other things, schools should:

[place] more emphasis on group projects and academic team competitions

[give] more student responsibility for discipline and the up-keep of the school building

[sponsor] more community service projects

[hold] more ceremonial activities such as assemblies and opening exercises that emphasize values that schools wish to promote, including cooperation, effort and patriotism

The character crisis in our country is also being felt in the marketplace. Employers are discovering that poor work habits and a lack of self-discipline pose even greater problems than missing skills. Some people suggest that at least some of the roots of unemployment in this country can be traced to home situations where children and youth have not learned to value respect, self-control, hard work, and delayed gratification.

No matter which crisis — in the marketplace, the classroom, or the courtroom — it can inevitably be traced back to the family and the very real acknowledgment that raising children today is harder than it used to be. Families of past generations who were constantly confronting survival issues had little opportunity to challenge values. Roles were more clearly defined and options limited. Dependency was real and conformity assumed. Values permeated all of life. Values taught in the home were reinforced by teachers, clergy, and the community. Accountability was built into the system, and outside influences were small.

THE TIMES HAVE CHANGED

The result of all these changes has been that many parents today are uncertain about what they believe and what they want their children to believe. Parents have become so fearful of being too prescriptive that they tolerate rather than teach. Freedom and self-expression have been encouraged at the expense of responsibility and self-control. Instead of clear, definitive values, parents often communicate ambiguous ones.

Schools have not been able to compensate for this void created in the home. Churches wonder if the time they have with children is adequate to make a real difference. And children often give greater credence to the messages they receive from the media, peer groups, and the marketplace than they do to the traditional values-transmitting institutions of family, church, and school. This is especially true in the case of the media and popular culture. An adolescent's peer group, for example, used to consist of a handful of other teenagers at his or her high school. Now it is at least national in scope and influence. Variant lifestyles receive almost instant exposure via movies, music, TV, videos, cable, and radio, and alternative values have crept into the mainstream mentality—values summed up by such phrases as 'get by,' 'who cares,' 'so what,' 'whatever,' and 'what's in it for me?'

Unfortunately, the world in which families live often reinforces some of these alternative values. How, for example, does one maintain pride in performance when there is no clear relationship between a job and its outcome or product? What does interdependence mean to someone who lives in a condominium? How does one learn respect for the land when one lives in a world of concrete and asphalt? What meaning do fairness and integrity have when public heroes possess neither? What responsibility does a person have to work for the greater good in a society that counsels freedom from guilt rather than forgiveness for wrongdoing?

Family talk-show psychiatrist Joseph Novello believes that the vacillation of values is the source of many of the difficulties families face today. He is so convinced that the situation is critical that he advises parents to go back to the beginning and redefine what values are important to them. What kind of people do they want their children to become? To get parents started, Novello suggests fifteen of what he considers to be typically American values, values that have played a part in the development of the family in our country:

1. Will and determination
2. Patriotism
3. Independence and self-reliance
4. Courage to do your best
5. Family
6. Respect for law and what's right
7. Respect for human rights and property rights
8. Hard work and productivity
9. Equality
10. Grace in victory and defeat
11. Ability to make choices
12. Charity
13. Roots
14. Ability to live with uncertainty
15. Courage to stand up for your beliefs.[10]

Perhaps Novello's motive in taking these values off the shelf, dusting them off, and suggesting them to parents is to try and give parents a fair shake against the values that have already gained the attention of their children and exposure of the media. Parents need not apologize for giving children firm guidelines and consistent, clearly articulated values that are reinforced by their own behavior. Parents need to be aware of these roots and communicate them before they can help children develop wings adequate for today's world.

MEETING THE MEDIA HALF-WAY

Even parents who have authenticated their basic beliefs and are trying to communicate these values in the home with honesty, confidence, and clarity find their impact diluted by one of the most powerful teachers of values—the media.

The ability of the media to influence, persuade, and teach is well-documented, not only through academic studies but experientially as well. It goes without saying that children take in what they see, hear, and experience—not unlike living VCRs. And frequently the pictures they record come from sources other than their parents. When children enter kindergarten, for example, they will already have watched more hours of TV than they will spend in a college classroom earning a bachelor's degree. Children spend more time watching TV than any other activity except sleeping. For preschoolers, this often means four hours or more of viewing a day. By high school graduation, a young person will have clocked in fifteen thousand hours of TV viewing. This is not surprising when one considers that, in the average household, the TV is on forty-four hours a week. According to author Thomas Lickonia, we have allowed TV "to replace us as our children's primary moral teacher."[11] If we add to TV viewing the time that children spend going to movies and watching videotapes and music videos—plus the time they spend listening to compact discs, tapes, and the radio—the amount of time during which young people are being influenced by the media is astounding.

This very media overload has not escaped media attention. Magazine articles explore the differences between the ways in which non-TV viewers and light viewers perceive the world as compared to heavy viewers. Newspaper columnists otherwise described as liberal declare that they've had it with the movies. Mothers lobby to have song lyrics printed on record albums, and books explore the problems of TV viewing. Television itself gets in on the act with public service announcements encouraging parents to keep TV in perspective. In some circles, it has even become a status symbol to declare oneself a non-viewer.

Such isolation would not prepare our children adequately for today's world. The world is, after all, very media-conscious. To completely prohibit TV or movie viewing is a setup for future problems. Children frequently covet most what they have been denied. There must be a middle ground, therefore, between those who would throw away the TV and those who exercise no control over it at all.

In fairness, TV and movies are not always negative influences. There are TV programs that are educational, inspirational, humorous, or just plain fun and relaxing to watch. Watching a movie or a TV show together can be a positive family activity and promote closeness. Certain movies and programs raise opportunities for parents and children to share opinions and discuss values. The TV can be a godsend for a sick child or a welcome diversion after a hectic, demanding day.

A balanced assessment of media influences on the family leads parents to the significant realization that they are not helpless. They have a lot of say about what media influences their children encounter, especially in the early years. Parents can decide, for example, when the TV is on, how many shows are watched, and which ones. Parents should decide, especially for preadolescents, which movies will be viewed, both in theaters and at home. There are guides available in most video stores to help parents make these judgments.

Parents can help their children strive for a balance of activities, including ones that are active, passive, intellectual, and creative. They can make sure that conversation, reading, and relationships are not sacrificed because of family viewing habits. They can resist the temptation to use the TV as a babysitter. They can make a point of watching certain movies with their children so that they have the opportunity to monitor the messages being conveyed. Some parents place the TV set in a little-used room to de-emphasize its role in family life. Other families circle shows in the *TV Guide* each week to limit the actual amount of viewing. Other parents choose to align themselves with activist groups seeking to change the ways values are conveyed by the media. The point is that parents are not powerless. They have far more control than they realize. Television has a place in the home, and it is the parents' job to define that place and maintain it.

Parents are not only becoming more aware of the responsibility they have to monitor messages from the media, but they are beginning to recognize the important role they play in teaching values to their children. Recently, a PTA in our area sent home a list of twenty-six free gifts parents can give their children, including beliefs, justice, kindness, reliability, and discipline. This list underscores the need for parents to define their values, what is really important to them, and then discuss these values clearly and intentionally in the home. Values should be the basis for decision-making as well as the operating guidelines for discipline. Values help define a family and at the same time give identity to the individuals who make up that family.

How Children Learn

Once comfortable with their own values, parents can then turn their attention to understanding how children learn values. Children, almost from birth, function as though they bring with them into the world a high-fidelity, stereophonic, living-color camcorder. They go about their days literally recording everything they see, hear, and experience—a videotape of life. They record it all. This fact was brought home to us when our children were small. Driving home from church one day, the three children were in the back seat and our daughter, who was very much 'into' Mary Poppins at the time, was singing a song from the album. Her singing was punctuated with periodic, well-timed, grating screeches. Finally, one of her younger brothers asked in frustration about the extra sound effects accompanying her singing. "Those," Lisa informed him emphatically, "are the scratches on the record." Children take it all in, even the scratches. They record what parents want them to notice and what parents wish they would overlook, and these recordings, available to children for later replay, become the raw materials from which values are formed.

Children record not only parents, siblings, relatives, teachers, and ministers, but also daycare personnel, babysitters, playmates, and models drawn from advertising, music, movies, and TV. Messages recorded early in life are more potent than those recorded after the child has developed the intellectual maturity to sort though the input and question, challenge, or compare it with past data. At an early age, children simply record what happens—what they hear and what they see—with little regard to right and wrong, good and bad, true and false. It is up to parents to help children make these distinctions. It is up to parents and other significant adults to help children make sense of all the recordings.

Despite increased competition for the attention of children in our society, parents remain the most significant and influential teachers of values, even if this potential goes unrealized in many families. It is the love and approval of parents and family that children need and value most highly, and their parents' example is the most important to children. After all, a TV set can't give a child a hug.

A book we have found helpful in understanding how children learn is Dr. Thomas Lickonia's *Raising Good Children*. Relying heavily on the work of Jean Piaget and Lawrence Kohlberg for help in understanding learning stages, Lickonia shows that moral development in children is also slow and in stages. Once parents recognize the stages of moral development that Lickonia describes, he then suggests parental responses and actions that either (a) go with the flow, or (b) challenge that stage's moral reasoning.

How Parents Teach

Insights into how children learn lead naturally into guidance for how parents teach. Parents often look for extraordinary opportunities as the most fertile ground for teaching values, but it is everyday life that presents parents with the best opportunities for teaching values. Values are best taught in simple, natural ways, when children watch what parents do and listen to what they say. Values are both visualized and verbalized. They are taught and caught. The time can be any time — in the car, at the grocery store, at church, or at home. The Old Testament writer of Deuteronomy understood this when he gave parents who wanted to teach their children the principles of God the following timeless advice:

> *Recite them to your children and talk about them when you are at home and when you are away, when you lie down and when you rise. Bind them as a sign on your hand, fix them as an emblem on your forehead, and write them on the doorposts of your house and on your gates.*
> Deuteronomy 6:7–9

Parents teach values, therefore, by what they do, what they say, and what they expect of their children. Most parents are aware of the ineffectiveness of telling children to 'do as I say, not as I do.' When what parents say and what they do are consistent, they enhance the opportunity for the value to be integrated. Too often there is a difference between the words and actions of parents, and children are more likely to tune in to the doing than the saying. They are perceptive at picking up and pointing out contradictory messages, especially as they enter adolescence. Mom may say, "Always tell the truth," but then she asks Dad to say she isn't home when someone she wishes to avoid calls on the phone. Dad may talk about honesty, but then he declares that a friend is eleven years old instead of twelve to get a reduced rate at the movies.

Most parents are aware of the importance of the parental model, although they don't always practice what they preach. Many parents today discount the parallel importance of the message. As Dr. Lickonia points out, "We must also preach what we practice." Parents teach not only by doing but by telling. Lickonia explains:

Kids are surrounded by bad examples. They need our words as well as our actions. They need to see us leading good lives. They also need to know why we do it. For our examples to have the maximum impact, they need to know the values and beliefs that are behind them.[12]

This doesn't mean that parents will have all the answers. That expectation is unfair to parents and its charade would be resented by kids. The problem today is that too many parents have *no* answers. Teaching values often requires parents walking children through the acceptable behaviors. It's a matter of the model, the message, and follow-through. If, for example, parents want children to learn fair play, consideration for others, and kindness, they teach these values by demonstrating them in family relationships. They explain why they are doing what they are doing and also teach as they walk their children through the behaviors those values imply:

"No, that cookie is for Sue."

"We take turns in our family."

"Dad is talking now. I will listen to you when he is done."

"I will not allow you to hurt Suzy, just as I do not allow Suzy to hurt you."

"Kittens are for loving. We pat them gently. Let me show you how. Now you show me."

"I know you want to go on the Teen Club ski trip, but we need the money for a valve job on the car. Is there any way you can earn the money yourself?"

To most effectively teach values to children, parents need to define their own values and what is important to them, understand how children learn and how parents teach, and then communicate their values through what they do, say, and expect with clarity, strength, integrity, and intentionality.

WINGS: A VALUES-AFFIRMING PROCESS

This is the best we can do. Parents sometimes need to remind themselves that the rest is up to their children. Children are the ones who must respond, learn, grow, and ultimately integrate values into their lives. This they must do for themselves. Parents cannot do it for them. After all, each generation will define its own values in a somewhat different fashion from the previous one. Some values children may discard, and others they may adapt. Most they will accept and teach to their children. Parents are responsible for guiding their children as best they know how throughout their growing-up years. When grown children make different values decisions, however, this is not necessarily a negative reflection on their parents. Too many parents torment themselves with guilt over decisions that their grown children make. For reasons that defy all logic, some children raised in homes where conscientious parents have given both love and discipline make decisions that bring pain to those they love as well as chaos to their own lives. Similarly, some children raised in homes with abusive, negligent parents grow up to become happy, productive, and useful citizens. There is a lot we cannot know about people and their predispositions. Also, some children simply seem unable to resist peer pressures that run counter to their parents' teachings. Parents can only be expected to apply what they know, do the best job they can, and find satisfaction in having done so.

Children, ultimately, become their own persons and must take responsibility for their lives and the decisions they make. Parents must learn to relinquish their propensities both to control and to rescue and allow children to assume responsibility and independence, to make mistakes their parents can no longer save them from, and to learn lessons their parents can no longer teach. Values conflicts between the generations are inevitable, but these gaps can be bridged when there is willingness by both parents and grown children to build on shared values and transcend differences with love.

3

Affection:
How Parents Care

If cohesion is the way parents help strengthen the family as a unit, affection is the means by which parents strengthen the individuals within the family. Affection does this by addressing feelings, but what role do feelings play in parenting? If recognition and reinforcement are so important, how can parents give children the opportunity to develop as positive a self-image as possible? How can parents give children the roots of self-respect and confidence and the capacity for love? To answer these questions will require honesty, resolution, and an appreciation of the real role affection plays in family life.

EXPECTATIONS AND SELF-IMAGES

When a baby is born, it is almost as if that child is handed the special assignment of figuring out the answers to three important questions: (1) Who am I? (2) Who are you? and (3) What are we doing here? The order in which these questions appear is no accident. The first challenge of childhood is development of an ego, a self-image, a sense of self-worth. Does one feel good about oneself? Does one like who one is? Does one think of oneself as competent? Important? Worthy of love? This sense of self-worth is less the product of what children bring with them (as important as these predispositions and potentialities may be) than it is the product of how they are treated:

Does someone want and welcome each child?

Does someone listen?

Does someone care?

Does someone love?

or

Is one considered a bother? A pain? A distraction?

Is one ridiculed? Hurt? Ignored? Abused?

By reading the signals and clues their parents send, children develop their own perceptions of how their parents feel about them. It is this felt image that is reflected back when children look at themselves in life's mirror.

As parents provide or fail to provide acceptance and affection and respond or fail to respond to feelings, so children frame positive or negative self-images. Indeed, this sense of self-worth is also shaped (at earlier and earlier ages) by other significant adults such as caregivers, daycare workers, and teachers, but parents remain the most valued source of approval, love, and good feelings.

Obviously, self-image isn't set in the first year, perhaps not even in the first ten. How others respond to a child's strengths and weaknesses and successes and failures throughout childhood is important. So also is the way children begin to assess themselves, but there is no better beginning in life than an early and strong sense of self-worth. These roots of self-confidence and self-respect are nurtured by the affection parents provide. Affection is the primary way in which parents can help children feel good about themselves.

When a child is welcomed into a loving family with genuine warmth and affection, that child feels important—valued and valuable. A cold, unresponsive reception results in feelings of worthlessness and failure. The hurt and pain or confidence and encouragement experienced in childhood are often carried throughout life.

Honor Whitney, a family therapist in Fort Worth, Texas, spent fifteen years researching the specific effects of destructive and constructive remarks on self-image. She concluded, somewhat predictably, that "negative statements seriously undermine the way people feel about themselves" and "positive, supportive statements have an equally strong effect on personality." Whitney developed a Self-Image Reinforcement (SIR) inventory that included the most common statements adults recalled hearing as children. Nine out of ten individuals cited the following comments as ones they considered destructive to their self-images:

How often do I have to tell you?

Do you expect me to believe that?

Look at you . . . you're a mess.

When are you going to grow up?

Can't you do anything right?

Now if that wasn't a stupid thing to say.

I guess I just can't trust you.[1]

Often the ways in which people relate to each other become self- fulfilling prophecies. A classic example is the film, *My Fair Lady* (based on George Bernard Shaw's play, *Pygmalian*), in which a cockney flower girl is transformed into a princess. Eliza Doolittle concludes that the difference between a flower girl and a princess "isn't who she is but how she's treated." Dramatic examples of negative self-fulfilling prophecies are often cited by people and groups whose achievement levels were limited, not by their potential, but by others' expectations of them. Positively or negatively, parents' expectations and expressions of those expectations shape their children's self-images and influence the kind of people they become.

Because self-images are so important, it is helpful to understand how they are developed in the first place. When William Wordsworth said that "the child is father of the man," he truly gave us an intimation of our immortality. History does repeat itself—if not in the cosmic events of our planet, at least in the personal events of our lives. Like father, like son. Like mother, like daughter. Like parent, like child. Most behaviors are learned from parents or other significant adults in one's life. Early self-images are primarily reflections of others' treatment of us and our feelings about that treatment at the time.

A SACK FULL OF FEELINGS

Most parents realize that children will inevitably acquire some negative feelings. Parents can talk about minimizing negative feelings or decide on behaviors to balance them, but they cannot eliminate them. How children handle these negative feelings and how parents provide for their reinforcement help define the early conditions for a child's self-image. The accumulation of a range of negative feelings—including hurt, anger, guilt, envy, fear, resentment, and inadequacy—becomes the basis for the burdens of childhood and the parameters of a self-worth.

It is as if children are issued a sack at birth in which to collect and carry the feelings they acquire about themselves. Some children are told a hundred times a day in as many different ways that they simply don't have what it takes to be a success in life. They don't eat right. They don't sleep right. They don't talk, walk, or even go to the bathroom right. They easily conclude that they are stupid, dumb, or ugly. Their sacks become filled with these and similar feelings. Obviously, not all children's sacks are equally burdensome. Each child's experience is unique. Each learns to cope by observing the models that their parents, siblings, and peers provide.

STRATEGIES

We have observed four common strategies people use to deal with diminished self-images. They are: Help! Hide! Hit! and Hype!

These strategies vary considerably as they manifest themselves in behavior, but all four are covert ways of seeking recognition, reassurance, or affirmation, and there is a deep and strong incentive for children to use them. It isn't difficult to see, however, that persistent reliance on these strategies as behavioral or communication norms (for a child or a family) will result in reinforcing negative self-images, undermining relationships, or eroding the foundation of affection and affirmation upon which families strive.

Strategy 1: Help!

Susie discovers that Mom is interested and sympathetic when she tells about an argument she had at school with her best friend Joan. Mom takes Susie's side, offering comfort and advice for the next time Joan treats her unkindly. At dinner, Mom tells the rest of the family about Susie's argument, and Susie again becomes the center of attention as family members express their sympathy and offer suggestions. Later in the evening, when Susie tells about a fun game she and Joan played at recess, Mom responds blandly.

If Mom's attention, sympathy, and support are more actively available when Susie is having problems than when things are going well, Susie may well conclude that she will receive more attention and recognition by having problems. This is not to suggest that parents shouldn't listen or identify with their children's difficulties, but children do tend to repeat behaviors that bring the most recognition from parents. Therefore, in homes where attention and recognition are given primarily for having problems, a relationship of dependency develops in which the child does not learn to trust her own judgment or solve her own problems. She may grow into an adult who also relates to others in this fashion.

To ask for help is one common way children learn to cope with feelings of low self-esteem by consistently looking to others for advice, reassurance, and decision-making. Children learn to believe that others are always more knowledgeable, skilled, or informed than they. Viewing life not as opportunities to be exploited but as burdens to be borne, such children become problem-oriented. Everything is seen as a problem or difficulty. They want, in effect, to find others to help them *carry the sack*. For such children, many relationships become defined in terms of the emotional support others give. As they grow older, the conclusion that the way to receive recognition is by having problems rather than by solving them is continually reinforced. The incentive for always needing help and advice is greater than the incentive for taking that advice or seeking real solutions to problems. This way of relating to others sets up a cycle that reinforces a child's feelings of inadequacy ("My problems are so bad that no matter what I do or who I ask, they won't improve"). It continually undermines self-esteem and eventually strains relationships if others tire of giving the advice that is seldom heeded.

Strategy 2: Hide!

When Michael misbehaves, he is immediately sent to his room. After a period of time, his parents invite him to rejoin the family. Little or no discussion follows about the incident that provoked the discipline. As Michael grows up, he frequently retreats to his room when he is worried, angry, or upset. He rarely talks about his feelings with others.

Michael is learning another way of coping with low self-esteem—by hiding feelings. People who rely on this response may assume that by remaining anonymous they will not risk exposure and judgment by others. They have learned to keep others at an emotional distance, and they seldom venture an opinion without consulting others first. Ralph Waldo Emerson's 'Trust yourself' is alien vocabulary. For these people, 'Protect yourself' is more appropriate. Although all people have times when they need to withdraw, the child who consistently relates to others in this fashion frequently becomes the adult who needs help with emotional and relationship problems. Used consistently, this pattern of behavior often signals the presence of deeper problems. To hide is another way children learn to *carry the sack* of negative feelings.

Strategy 3: Hit!

Anthony is upset with himself because he has not scored as many baskets for his team as he'd hoped. When Jumar, one of his teammates, is fouled, Anthony charges, "We may as well forfeit the game. Jumar couldn't hit a free throw if his life depended on it."

The third (and possibly the most popular) way children learn to handle negative feelings is this hitting option. They observe their parents and thousands of media models strike out (figuratively, if not literally) when they feel threatened, vulnerable, or insecure. They observe others pointing the finger or attacking to turn attention away from themselves and their inadequacies. They hope to feel better by making others feel worse. This behavior is frequently encouraged among adolescents, and each generation finds different labels for such comments—*slams*, *put-downs*, *burns*, or *joning*, to mention just a few. The hit strategy is also modeled for children by people in positions of authority, where power or position provide a certain sanction to such behavior. Correcting errors, for example, is a legitimate function of authority, but when an error becomes the excuse to indict the *person* rather than to correct the behavior or improve the performance, the hit option is in action.

When striking out at others becomes a regular pattern of behavior and communication in a family, modeled by the parents and practiced by the children, the home becomes a battlefield instead of a haven. Ultimately, this pattern can undermine a marriage, warp the behavior of all the children, and destroy communication among the entire family.

Strategy 4: Hype!

In conversations about the schools in her community, Mrs. Collins maneuvered every discussion to the program for gifted children in which her children participated. She always mentioned how well her children had scored on the program's prerequisite tests.

Mia won two first-place ribbons in the 4-H fair. Her friend Effie did not place with her entries. When Effie came to visit, Mia displayed her blue ribbons where Effie would be sure to see them.

The Bronsons were planning a party, and one of the guests was a camera enthusiast who frequently entered free-lance photos in amateur contests. Mr. Bronson's photographic interests were primarily limited to informal family situations, but before the party he traded in his camera for a more expensive, sophisticated model.

In this fourth pattern for dealing with low self-esteem, children learn from parents and other models to manipulate their conversations and the environment to impress others and promote themselves. This extends far beyond an appropriate acknowledgment and appreciation of their own talents, abilities, and achievements. With this behavior pattern, children learn to proclaim their skills in order to achieve status. They become more interested in the symbols of success and esteem than in their substance. For adults who rely on this strategy of relating, the degrees after their name, for example, ultimately become more important than the knowledge those degrees represent and the opportunities they provide.

For adults and children, there is a difference between self-rejection, self-acceptance, and self-proclamation. The first means being doubtful of one's accomplishments and uncertain of one's value; the second means being at peace with the gifts one possesses and eager to share them appropriately; and the third means to give priority to promotion, with the basis for the boast being secondary. The following examples illustrate these three behavior patterns:

A friend comments, "I like your dress."

Self-rejection:	"This old thing?"
Self-acceptance:	"Thanks. I did, too."
Self-promotion:	"I like anything from Saks 5th Avenue."

A father asks his son, "Who would like to try this new computer program?"

Self-rejection:	"Those things are too hard for me."
Self-acceptance:	"I would."
Self-promotion:	"Let me be first. I can figure out anything."

Children who learn to handle low self-esteem with hype frequently view others' successes as being at their expense. Their achievements are seen as another's losses. Sometimes transparent, sometimes subtle and sophisticated, this strategy is also sometimes culturally sanctioned. From scramblings for political power to manipulation for economic and social gain, the hype response is a learned failure to relate to others in an honest, open, and straightforward fashion. Ultimately, the greatest cost is to the individual who never learns that the rewards of power and status born of manipulation and used solely for self-promotion are short-lived. *Real* self-esteem comes from the substance of achievement and the commitment and caring of relationships.

All parents find themselves slipping from time to time into one of these nonconstructive ways of handling feelings of low self-esteem. It is only when these strategies become the preferred patterns of communicating and relating that they undermine children's personal effectiveness and endanger their future relationships.

COPING WITH SACKS

The most hope for teaching and learning constructive ways of handling negative feelings exists within the family. The family is the ideal place to initiate long-term societal change. Families can not only produce changed individuals, but they can also shape the cycle for future generations. The family offers the best setting to think, talk, teach, and act differently. Rather than perpetuate past problems, families can teach new patterns and send

Common Ways of Carrying Sacks

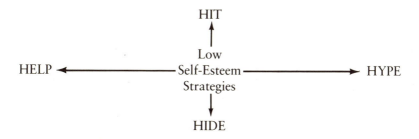

forth individuals prepared to transform their potential into performance. Parents give children roots that include models of positive ways of handling negative feelings and the wings of practice.

As families and individuals give each other—freely and directly—the affection and emotional support that all people require, the need to maneuver and manipulate others in order to receive that affection is reduced. Parents can do this by recognizing, accepting, and then positively and intentionally compensating for the inevitable negative feelings that contribute to low self-esteem. It is a three-step process.

Recognize

First, parents must recognize that childhood is not, and probably should not be, anxiety-free. Concerns, worries, doubts, fears, and feelings of inadequacy are inevitable parts of growing up. Children are, after all, small in a world of big people. This size difference alone reinforces feelings of helplessness. Our youngest son, who is adopted, came to us at age one from Vietnam. Smaller than his peers, Tim helped us appreciate a child's perspective. We couldn't understand his fear of dogs until we realized that when the next-door neighbor's dog peered through the fence, Tim's eyes were at the same level as the dog's teeth. And once, during a Christmas season, we took all three of our children to a crowded shopping mall. Tim, who was holding Gary's hand, suddenly began crying for no apparent reason. When Gary knelt down to comfort him, he saw the world from Tim's perspective—hundreds of knees coming at him from all directions! Being a child is sometimes scary.

Dependency is real. Children must rely completely upon the big people in their lives to provide what they need for physical survival—food, clothing, and shelter—as well as to meet the emotional needs that are essential to psychological well-being. For most children these needs are adequately met, and a sense of security is created. For some children these needs are largely unmet, and the result is physical and emotional deprivation. Even in the best of environments, children may conclude that dependency is a less-than-desirable state of affairs. Children are praised and encouraged for doing things all by themselves. Growing up is the process of developing this independence.

Not only do children experience feelings of inadequacy from being little, helpless, and dependent, but they also experience such feelings as a direct result of what their parents do and say. Parents themselves become the source of some of these feelings as they seek to protect their children from harm and teach them appropriate behaviors that are consistent with their values.

Children are self-centered. They want what they want now. However, their needs and wants cannot always prevail. They must learn to wait. They think of themselves first, but they must learn to consider others. They act on impulse, but they must learn to consider consequences. Parents have a responsibility to teach and control, and that is a necessary but sometimes painful process for both parties. When children are corrected or disciplined, they will most likely feel hurt, inadequate, resentful, guilty, or angry. To some extent, such feelings are an inevitable part of childhood. All children grow up with some negative feelings about themselves and others in their sacks.

Not only are parents the source of some of these negative feelings but so are neighborhood and school peers and other people that children encounter. Even if it were possible for parents to produce a completely positive environment in the home, external contacts would quickly dilute the euphoria. What happens to children outside the home, both positive and negative, becomes part of their unique experience. It is a constant challenge for parents to balance the need to be protective with the need to let children gain skills and confidence by coping successfully on their own.

ACCEPT

Once parents recognize that negative feelings are a normal part of family life, they can accept these feelings for what they are — neither overreacting nor discounting their significance. Children need to know that everyone feels hurt, angry, disappointed, or upset sometimes. Parents also have difficult relationships, all people experience failure, and no one is good at everything. There is, however, a difference between having negative feelings and acting them out in unacceptable ways. Parents must help children learn positive ways of handling their negative feelings, ways that do not result in their dumping on others. And even though parents should monitor children's negative behaviors, they should also encourage children to share their negative feelings. Feelings are not facts, and parents need to realize that. Feelings may be self-centered, illogical, and unfair. They are often transitory, but they are *real*, and parents must deal with this reality to help children convert negative feelings and experiences into constructive behaviors. Of course, parents already send messages about how or how not to do exactly that by the ways in which they handle feelings themselves. When children see parents expressing their feelings, they gain permission to do likewise.

If parents can help children learn to discuss negative feelings one at a time rather than letting them build up, their children will have mastered a powerful skill for improving not only their emotional well-being but their relationships as well. It is when negative feelings are consistently kept private that they have the most power. In the home, parents can help children talk about their feelings and examine what's in their sacks in a safe environment. They can then encourage and help their children to do whatever is possible to improve the situation that resulted in the bad feelings and then discard their ill will and get on with life.

COMPENSATE

If negative feelings are inevitable, what about positive ones? What about the conversations and accomplishments that help children feel good about themselves? What about the feelings and experiences that reinforce self-esteem and self-confidence? Do all children have a reservoir of good feelings, too?

Unfortunately, this doesn't seem to be the case. Although most children acquire good feelings along the way to adulthood, they are sometimes only serendipitous. Positive feelings in childhood often have a way of getting lost in the averages. The family, however, is in a uniquely fortuitous position when it comes to feelings. It is able to overcome this disparity by laying a foundation of positive emotional support and affection for its members. The family can consciously and positively compensate by helping each child receive the emotional support necessary to reinforce a strong self-image. Rather than being a burden, good feelings can be enabling. Unlike the negative feelings that drag children down, good feelings energize them. Like a highly charged battery, positive feelings empower. They help children feel good, confident, self-assured, and enthusiastic about life — attitudes that contribute to success. And success in turn reinforces a positive self-image.

The good news is that the family can create situations in which children can acquire these good feelings. Negative feelings will still be there — those invoked by parental control and discipline as well as those originating outside the family — but parents can place the negative feelings within a strong, positive setting. This foundation of support and positive feelings is built, first and foremost, in a multitude of everyday situations as parents express affection to their children and help them feel good about who they are and the contributions they make to the family. These situations may involve the whole family as a unit, or they may be tailor-made activities targeted at helping a specific child feel important and special. Sometimes these experiences become significant emotional events in a child's life and will later be recalled as times of special growth or happiness. Such experiences might include:

an outing with Mom and Dad to celebrate a child's graduation from sixth grade.

a father-and-son fishing trip to talk about what it means to be a man, as well as what it takes to catch a fish!

a week-long visit with grandparents.

a religious retreat attended by a parent and child together.

a special vacation.

Such experiences can increase opportunities for closeness and the sharing of good feelings that will be retained in a reservoir of good will and positive memories and later recalled to help individuals and families through tough times.

Both the everyday and the extraordinary are important. The point is that parents need to go out of their way to create situations in which children can acquire feelings of competence, confidence, and self-worth.

Coping with Sacks

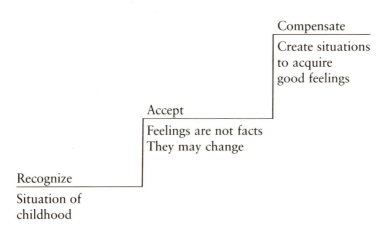

Compensate

Create situations
to acquire
good feelings

Accept

Feelings are not facts
They may change

Recognize

Situation of
childhood

BUILDING COMPETENCE

Growing up is not only a developmental process but also a discovery process. Children begin at an early age to try to figure out what they do well. It often seems to parents that children's interests bear little resemblance to the skills they will need to succeed as adults. The nursery school and elementary set often measure might by muscle (who can run fastest and jump highest), not an attribute that usually results in career payoffs. By junior high, social considerations become paramount, with organized sports or cheerleading often replacing small group activities.

Young children tend to be equally open to opportunities for proficiency in all areas—academic, physical, and social. This troubles some parents who are concerned that their children are not giving enough attention to the skills needed in a rapidly changing world. There is a very real maturity lag among boys, for example, and parents sometimes fear that by the time they get serious, they may already be too far behind in the acquisition of skills and knowledge. There is also much cause for concern as many of today's high school graduates leave secondary school less well-educated than their parents did.[2]

Many parents find themselves caught in the middle between a desire to see that their children are adequately prepared and a recognition that children also need protecting. Children are not mini-adults, and each has his or her developmental clock. Attempts to ignore the developmental process often backfire, and children rebel against too much pressure to excel.

On the other hand, parents also recognize that many children have been conditioned to expect instant gratification. Television, with its quick solutions to complicated problems, reinforces this expectation. Many children are accustomed to being entertained constantly; they are spectators. They have not yet learned such virtues as patience, perseverance, delayed gratification, and the willingness to work and struggle.

How can parents help children feel good about themselves as they discover and develop their unique strengths, gifts, and skills? First, parents can help by being themselves and sharing who they are with their children. Parents who enjoy reading are likely to read to their children, and those children are in turn likely to enjoy reading. Parents who are good at math may play math games with their children, and those children not only discover that math can be fun, but they begin to think of themselves as good in math, too. When Mom enjoys playing tennis, she teaches her child to play. Parents who like working with their hands will probably work on building projects with their children. When parents encourage children to participate in activities they themselves enjoy, their enthusiasm is contagious, and children are likely to develop competencies and interests similar to their parents'. An example of this was recently shared by a good friend whose grandchild brought home his first kindergarten drawing. It was of the town's water system; his parents are both engineers.

Children will also be interested in activities other than those their parents enjoy, however, and it is important for parents to respect their children's interests that differ from their own. By doing so, parents communicate to their children that it is all right to be an individual. It is acceptable to have different skills and interests, and these can enrich the experiences of the entire family. Parents may feel threatened, for example, when a child decides that soccer is more to his liking than the violin, even though his father played in the college orchestra. Or a girl may choose ballet lessons instead of gymnastics when her mother had been on the tumbling team. When parents pressure children—even if only by how they express their approval—to conform to their own interests, they are likely to invite resentment instead of compliance, if not immediately, then at some point in the future. A parent willing to compromise a little by cutting back on piano lessons during the soccer season may allow that child an opportunity to discover that his or her own talents are more musical than muscular.

Finally, there is growing recognition that children can learn as much (if not more) from free time as from structured activities. When our children were babies, many parents purchased walkers, devices that enabled easy movement. The babies could stay clean, skip crawling, and graduate earlier into those first solo steps. Only later did experts begin to speculate that babies learned many valuable lessons from crawling—pulling up, falling down, and judging distance—that later might even affect their reading skills. This is not to denigrate the importance of structured activities—from boys' and girls' clubs, to day camp, to lessons, to tennis clinics, to the popular computer camps. These activities can be valuable uses of time, not only for children but also for dual-career parents who are constantly challenged to arrange constructive ways to occupy their children. Sometimes, however, children's lives can become so structured—even with good activities—that they miss important opportunities to learn by filling their time with self-initiated and imaginative play. The importance of free play is often discounted. One psychologist[3] pointed out that play is a child's most important work. Children who learn to use imagination and creativity in play develop aspects of themselves that will be of infinite value. A child who has learned to read for enjoyment will never be bored. Perseverance and patience can be developed through woodworking projects or model building. A firsthand knowledge of simple machines comes from taking an old clock apart and then putting it back together. Children who devise their own games develop social skills. When our children were little, they especially enjoyed creating costumes to help them become cowboys, knights, astronauts, doctors, dragons, or cooks. When our niece (then in junior high) found herself with extra time one summer, she and a friend co-produced a neighborhood newspaper that they wrote, typed, and sold.

Children don't develop competencies solely through school and formal, structured activities but also through opportunity, encouragement, and freedom for unstructured learning and creative play provided in the home. As children develop their skills and strengths, they will discover that what they do will help them feel good about themselves.

BUILDING CONFIDENCE

Not only do parents need to set aside opportunities or set up situations for children to develop imagination, acquire skills, and gain proficiency, they also need to help their children develop confidence. At first appearance, it seems that the road to confidence is a chancy one, subject to some fortuitous acquisition of success experiences. What parent is not pleased when a child scores the winning touchdown, places first in a recital, or is chosen class president? Parents value these experiences not only out of pride, but primarily because of the recognition given their children. Parents can't manufacture these kinds of successes for their children, but when they come along, are understandably pleased.

The development of confidence, however, isn't solely—or even inevitably—the consequence of success. Children will not succeed at everything they do. Neither did their parents, although by the time they are grown, most people have narrowed the arenas in which they participate, eliminating those in which they will likely fail. A child may just miss being picked for the lead in the play, or lose the election for class treasurer by one vote, or not be nominated at all. He may get cut from first-string football or be demoted to second-chair clarinet. Only a small percentage of high-school students are inducted into the National Honor Society, and even fewer become National Merit finalists. Some children's performance in their best school subjects does not compare to other children's performance in their worst subjects. Although few parents want to acknowledge it, half of all children test below average. And only one person can win the blue ribbon in any event.

Society's judgments will be reality-based. After all, standards of achievement in our nation need raising. It is interesting to reflect, however, that some characteristics that correlate most clearly with success are not always measured on competency tests. Success in college math, for one example, does not always correlate to high scores on the math tests for college entrance. Confidence, motivation, perseverance, creativity, and the need to contribute can frequently propel a person of lesser ability and potential to greater heights of contribution and achievement than those judged early to have natural gifts and abilities. Parents need to remind themselves and their children that not all of life's winners come in first. The world needs more good band members than band directors. Physical therapists are needed as well as doctors. Professional careers are not endless ladders, and individuals who bring this expectation with them are programmed for disappointment. Competence is needed at every station. Parents must give their children a sense of place and contribution, not merely the desire for dominance and triumph. Parents should leave it to professional football coaches to maintain that winning is the only thing. Their job is to produce champions; a parent's job is to raise human beings who contribute to society.

Neither are society's so-called winners always the most confident, well-adjusted citizens. A string of Ph.D.s does not automatically assure high self-esteem, and even thousands of hands clapping may not be sufficient to bolster the ego of some people. The escalating rate of teen suicide, especially among bright, high-achieving students, says something about the pressures they perceive. Success as the world measures it does not necessarily go hand-in-hand with self-confidence.

How, then, can parents help build confidence in children? It seems to us that there are several important things parents can do. First, let children know that it is okay to lose. Mistakes and defeats are important parts of the learning process. Failure is, after all, only temporary — unless one lets it become permanent. In a science experiment, one learns by repeated failures, by trying again and again in a safe environment (the science classroom or laboratory) until one gets it right. The home, too, can be a place where one learns by failing, by trying again and at last succeeding. These experiences can act as fertile soil for the growth of confidence as children learn that mistakes and failures are inevitable parts of growing and learning. Children need to know that parental love, approval, and affection are not contigent upon winning.

A second way parents can help children develop confidence is by maintaining a growth distance. Some parents so over-identify with their children that they act as if their children's successes and failures were in fact their own. For example, a mother might feel as if the low grade on the report card were her own. Or a father might feel as if it were himself and not his son striking out with the bases loaded in the bottom of the ninth. Such over-identification can keep us from tuning in to our children's actual reactions, and it often causes parents to magnify hurt and defeat way out of proportion. Parental disappointment may make the defeat seem insurmountable to the child; not only has he failed, but he has let Mom and Dad down in the process. A low-key, the-world-keeps-on-turning attitude can help children put failures behind them and try again.

A third way parents encourage self-confidence in children is by having realistic expectations. There is a difference between a child's best and perfection. There may even be a difference between a child's best and the parents' best. Parents must adjust their expectations to the age, experience, maturity, and motivation of their children. Children are learning many things that parents have already mastered; sometimes parents forget how time-consuming their own growth has been. Even adults need to remind themselves that there is a difference between excellence and perfection. The pursuit of excellence may be a worthy goal, but the pursuit of perfection is a charade. When the only performances rewarded with praise are the ones that fully satisfy parents' extremely high standards, parents can convince children that they are working primarily to please adults. The child may not buy into the success for himself. External motivation tends to be short-lived, satisfied by the grade on the report card, the dollars for the As, or the praise for the job. But real motivation is internal, and one goal of child-rearing is to help children make the transition from working only to please others to pleasing themselves as well.

Finally, parents help build confidence by communicating to their children that success is a process, a series of steps. Children may be challenged by a long-range goal, but the steps along the way are important and require encouragement and recognition in and of themselves.

The movement from roots to wings is, after all, an incremental one. Parents provide and children experience. Parents encourage and children attempt. Parents model roots, and children, through successes and failures and repeated attempts, develop wings. Children's wings are developed through the process of taking initiative by internalizing the past and acting appropriately in the present. Children see the parental model, receive encouragement, and try something on their own.

BUILDING SELF-WORTH

Competence and confidence contribute to one's sense of self-worth. People feel better about themselves when they are comfortable with their accomplishments and potential, but self-worth has less to do with performance than with perception. A sense of self-worth is influenced mainly by one's understanding of how others see one. The view of others becomes a mirror in which people see themselves reflected, especially in their early years. Do others find them lovable? Do others enjoy being with them? Do others express positive feelings toward them? Parents can help children develop a positive sense of self-worth with the affection, recognition, and acceptance they convey.

This need in all people for recognition, affection, and emotional support is well-documented. It is essential to the physical development of children as well as their psychological well-being. It is important for adults as well. People of all ages seek positive recognition from others, but they often accept (perhaps even expect) negative when the positive is consistently unavailable. After all, negative attention is preferable to no attention at all.

How families meet this most basic of all human needs—the need for loving attention—helps determine each individual's sense of self-worth. When most people think of positive reinforcement, they think of praise or rewards for behavior—what is said to children, for example, when they are being good or meeting expectations:

"I appreciate your setting the table."

"You really got the car clean."

"Glad you emptied that wastebasket before supper."

This kind of performance-based praise can be an effective tool in teaching and discipline. Children, however, need not only praise for performance, but they also need acceptance that is not contingent upon behavior at all. Praise and criticism are conditional reinforcements: they are based upon doing. The aim of each is to get results—in the case of praise, a continuation of the desirable behavior. The aim of criticism is to evoke change. Both praise and criticism are ways of applying the merit system to families. Outside the home, much of one's time is spent living according to merit systems. Students go to school and receive grades based upon their performance. Adults go to work and receive payment, praise, or promotions based upon their performance.

The merit system has a place in family life as well, but families do not live by the merit system alone. The family is much more than a conditional organization. Individuals don't quit, flunk, get fired, or drop out of families. Despite the attention that must be given to behavior, affection and acceptance in families have to be unconditional or free—not purchased with performance or bartered for by behavior. Children are loved and accepted in families not because of what they *do* but simply because they *are*. Such unconditional acceptance is an application of the theological concept of grace in a family setting. Family members do not earn each other's love; love is freely given.

It is interesting to observe that the value children are likely to place on parents' conditional comments—advice, criticism, and praise—is directly related to the value they place on their unconditional reinforcement. Do parents really care? Do they listen? Are they open? Do they like their children as well as love them? Can they forgive? A child's sense of self-worth is strengthened in homes that freely give this unconditional love and acceptance. An important way parents do this is through the affection they provide. What, then, are some specific ways in which parents can express affection to children?

TOUCHING

Parents communicate affection by touching. Although parents are rightly concerned about the inappropriate touching associated with abuse, appropriate touching is important to the emotional well-being of people of all ages. For babies and small children, touching is essential to health and emotional development. Babies can actually die from lack of holding and touching even if their other physical needs are met. Recent research has suggested that many elderly people in nursing homes also suffer from the same deprivation symptoms neglected infants display. 'Have you hugged your kid today?' bumper stickers are right on target. Kids of all ages need hugging.

Some people do not feel comfortable being demonstrative, either physically or verbally. Raised in homes that de-emphasized the physical displays of affection, they become convinced that it just doesn't feel right for them. When they express affection, they feel phony or artificial, so they hold back. People feel comfortable when they are behaving as they have learned to behave. Unless they decide differently, they tend to behave in accordance with the values and behaviors learned a long time ago. Often these old behaviors work well; other times they may need to be changed. To decide to do things differently is always an act of will, and new ways of responding will feel uncomfortable at first. It is only after one has tried a new behavior on for size and practiced using it that it becomes comfortable. Many people are simply unwilling to weather the transition period required in order for feelings to catch up with actions.

It is helpful to think of change as a process. One begins with the status quo—where one is now. A parent may behave in ways that, although appropriate in other times and places, are not working well in the here and now. That parent may not even be aware of how behaviors, attitudes, or feelings could be compromising his or her effectiveness. For example, a parent may not be noticing opportunities to recognize a child with a pat on the back, a hug, or an encouraging word. Then, suddenly or slowly, the parent reaches the conclusion that change is needed. Perhaps he takes a class or reads a book or suffers a relationship crisis that brings his own shortcomings to his attention. This realization is often painful because, even though the person now notices the ways in which he falls short, he is not yet able or willing to change. This level of awareness is the goal of consciousness-raising. The problem with consciousness-raising is that is might stall out at that stage. What the parent needs to do next is develop and practice new and more appropriate ways of responding. Then change begins. Now he not only notices the times when a hug would be appreciated, but he gives the hug, even if that behavior is an uncharacteristic one. At the same time, he is consciously aware of responding differently and may even feel uncomfortable, awkward, and a little phony. Sometimes his discomfort is perceived by others, who notice the awkwardness. Other people may even inadvertently or unconsciously try to push the person back into old patterns of behavior, not because the old ways of behaving are preferable, but because they are predictable. People cope best with what is familiar, and that is a large part of what makes change so difficult. Many people simply give up at this point, but if the parent hangs in there long enough, he begins to develop not only skill, but also ease, as he integrates these new patterns into his behavior. They become comfortable to him and others, and he can now emphatically proclaim, "That's the new me!"

A couple of cautions are in order. Change is appropriate in situations where one is having trouble, where behaviors are not working well. Of the thousands of programmed responses each of us has, most work fairly well. It helps to acknowledge the many ways in which people relate effectively to others as well as the ways that need change and improvement. The other implication is for parenting. The more able parents are to teach children information that is accurate and behavior that is applicable, the easier the acquisition of wings will be. One of the problems with this goal is that the world is changing rapidly: despite the best intentions of parents, children will constantly be faced with the need to re-examine what they have learned. As parents model processes for change in their own lives, they pass on this model for change to their children, and these processes become roots.

Finally, recognizing change as a process helps one understand why not feeling like it is no excuse for unwillingness to change when change is needed. And it is no excuse for parents' failure to provide the affection children need. We once heard theologian Karl Michaelson struggling with why it is that people do not do the deeds of love even when they know they are the right things to do. He concluded that it is not necessary for the deeds of love to wait for the feeling. People do not need to feel loving to be loving. Surprisingly, when one acts loving, the feelings have a way of catching up. All it takes is the will to practice, practice, practice.

Parents Communicate Affection by Talking

Words are one of the best ways individuals have of letting others know they care. The problem is that some people simply assume that those close to them should know of their love without their actually having to verbalize it. Cathy's cartoon boyfriend, Irving, struggles with a similar assumption as he addresses a valentine to his mother. When a friend points out that he ought to write 'I love you,' Irving protests, "We don't have the kind of relationship where I actually have to say I love her!"[4] Even though we know others love us, we need to hear the words. It helps to know that others notice and appreciate us. We once conducted a marriage seminar in which couples were instructed to spend ten minutes taking turns completing the following statement to each other: "I appreciate in you . . . " So unaccustomed were many of them to telling their spouses what they specifically loved and appreciated that the exercise became an ordeal instead of an opportunity. In a curious sort of way, sometimes people withhold complimenting others because they feel it as some sort of loss for themselves. To be more appreciative of someone else than that person is of you makes some people feel vulnerable. It is easy to see how destructive these attitudes can become in close relationships. Parents need to communicate their affection in families by what they *say*.

Parents Communicate Affection by Doing

Parents communicate affection by doing as well as by saying. They must customize their deeds as well as their comments to reinforce a child's sense of self-worth. They need to look actively for ways to express affection toward family members through actions. A song that appeared on the pop charts included the refrain, "You don't send me flowers anymore." In some homes, expressing affection may call for sending flowers again. In other homes, it may mean a special favor. One of our friends says that the action she most appreciates is when her husband does the dishes if she has a meeting. Finding out what others appreciate most and doing it can bring a real sense of personal satisfaction in addition to success in relationships. It may mean notes left in lunchboxes, a trip to the library to check out a book needed for a school assignment, or help with household chores. It may mean fixing a favorite dessert for the person who has just taken a difficult test or returned from a tiring trip. It may mean saving an article or a cartoon that a particular person would enjoy. College students especially need reminders that they are still important to the family—through letters, telephone calls, newspaper clippings, and surprise care packages.

We found that surprises are often especially effective ways of expressing affection. During the teen years, when some adolescents may become embarrassed with overt parental affection (especially in front of friends), carefully selected surprises offer additional opportunities to say a child is important. Little children, of course, thrive on surprises. When our children were young, out of the well-established tooth fairy tradition grew a whole host of fairies who left surprises at the breakfast table, ranging from erasers and Life Savers to bubble gum and lip gloss. Imagine our delight one Christmas to find on our desks pencil containers full of peppermint treats, mysteriously left for us by the candy cane fairy. When parents set the example, children will also enjoy looking for ways to express their affection in actions. Surprises can help keep family life exciting. They are a break in the routine, a special way of showing through deeds that we care about those close to us. Being affectionate is truly a show-and-tell experience.

PARENTS COMMUNICATE AFFECTION BY WAITING

T-shirts that declare "God isn't done with me yet" tell it all. People of all ages are in the process of becoming, and children especially need parents who can sometimes overlook the setbacks and give them time to figure things out for themselves. Because growing up is a process of becoming self-responsible, it is never all smooth sailing—for parents or children. A little room for grace is needed by parents who recognize what the author of a delightful musical play affirmed:

> Kids under construction
> Maybe the paint is still wet
> Kids under construction
> The Lord might not be finished yet.[5]

PARENTS COMMUNICATE AFFECTION BY LISTENING

One of the most positive ways a parent can communicate affection to a child is by listening, not only to the words but also to the feelings behind the words. Most Americans actually listen with only about 25 percent attentiveness. What is it that prevents parents from actually listening to their children?

One reason parents have trouble listening is that they are too preoccupied with their own agendas to tune in to their children. People concentrate on what they are going to say rather than what another person is saying. If you doubt this, ask yourself how many times you have been introduced to somebody only to discover minutes later that you have forgotten that person's name? This same tendency causes parents to discount their children.

Sometimes parents don't listen very well because of assumptions they make. Certain words, people, or situations become triggers, invoking responses that are more tied up in the past than tuned in to the present. Parents sometimes respond the same way their parents responded years ago in similar situations, without stopping to really hear the unique concerns and feelings of their children today.

A third reason for poor listening by parents is a desire many have to come up with solutions for every problem and advice for every situation. Many parents want to judge or solve rather than listen to children's reactions, feelings, and thoughts. In addition, parents often want to make points or balance things out rather than to listen with sensitivity and give a child the opportunity to solve her own problems. Because there are differences between listening for facts, values, and feelings, parents especially need to learn how to tune in to feelings because of their importance in families. There is no substitute for genuine interest by parents which manifests itself in a willingness to listen and empathize. When parents are ready listeners, children know they care.

PARENTS COMMUNICATE AFFECTION BY LAUGHING

As families share what is fun and funny, they give children permission through model and practice to develop one of the most creative ways to handle stress, promote healthfulness, and express affection. A sense of humor is probably one of the most neglected resources parents have at their disposal.

Of course, the kind of humor we are recommending is not sarcasm or one that derives its mirth at the expense of another person. It is a humor that can be shared and enjoyed. It is a humor that helps put things in perspective and prevents overreaction to life's seriousness. It is a humor that allows one to laugh as one makes mistakes, learns, and grows.

Family humor and laughter can break tension, reduce stress, create cohesion, and teach us about life. Television's popular "Cosby Show" offered many examples of how humor can teach values and discipline and build family rapport—not only for the Huxtables but for all of families.

One of the rewards of parenting is watching children's developing sense of humor as they experience roots and develop wings. Very small children tend to laugh at whatever others find funny, especially responding to exaggerated gestures and facial expressions. As parents share funny stories, books, songs, movies, or TV shows with their children, children begin to develop a sense of what makes something humorous. Children love to try out jokes on others, especially adults who laugh at them all (although, perhaps, with a little more vigor at the ones that are truly funny). School-age children may enjoy joke books or calendars that include a joke for every day of the year. They also like to tell their families about the funny things that happen at school. It is interesting to watch children progress not only through different levels of humor but also through recurrent joke types such as good news/bad news jokes or knock-knock jokes. Adolescents, with their capacity for understanding and appreciating more sophisticated forms of humor such as word games, irony, and puns are often delightfully adept at interjecting a humorous dimension into ordinary family conversations.

Each family develops its own set of what our children call 'location jokes,' the ones you have to have been there to appreciate, and these humorous incidents become part of a family's folklore and promote cohesiveness. An episode of the popular TV show, "Family Ties," revolved around what were called 'Alex jokes,' with family flashbacks that focused on funny situations in which Alex had found himself in prior episodes. Some 'location' jokes derive their humor from their obvious hyperbole.

When our son Tim was fifteen, he reduced us to laughter one dinnertime by boldly challenging, "Ask me anything. I know everything about history up to World War II." Other times, the timing is the secret. During a station break in one of Tim's favorite TV programs, he whipped out a copy of John Steinbeck's *The Pearl* (which he'd been reading for English class), grabbed a pencil and paper and asked, "Real quick, Mom, before the commercial ends, what makes *The Pearl* a classic?"

Sometimes the unexpected creates humor. Our son Christopher, whose favorite sport is fishing, was telling us about a school assignment in which the class had to write a composition of comparison and contrast. "Boy, some of the kids in that class are so unoriginal," he announced. "They couldn't think of anything more interesting to compare than a dog and a cat." He continued, "As for me, I really got into it. Mine was good. I compared and contrasted a catfish and a bass." This is the same young man who expressed relief that the bookmobile hadn't turned in front of us in the school parking lot because all he had was his learner's permit, and "They would have thrown the book at me." Chris also comforted us when a guest speaker was late arriving for a class we'd organized at church. "If the teacher doesn't arrive," we asked him, "do you think you could tell the class jokes for one hour?" "No," Chris answered, without missing a beat. "But I could tell one joke and they'd laugh for an hour."

Humor also can be premeditated. On one of our trips west, Gary discovered a brand of chewing gum called Bianca. It became a game for him to purchase a pack on the sly and try to conceal it from the children. The kids, however, acquired a superhuman ability to sniff out a new package and chant, "Bianca gum! Bianca gum! Bianca gum!" until Gary, with a feigned show of reluctance, would share his purchase. Upon our return home from this trip, we noticed that the last package of Bianca gum was missing from Gary's dressertop. In its place, in our daughter Lisa's handwriting, was the first of in a series of ransom notes.

These are some humorous stories our family remembers. Each family develops its own legacy of humor. Humor is an invaluable family resource. It allows families to affirm each other as fun to be with, and it is a way of expressing affection.

PARENTS COMMUNICATE AFFECTION BY FORGIVING

If all kids are truly "under construction," then family life needs an element of grace that recognizes that all people make mistakes, precipitate accidents, are sometimes grouchy, or say unkind things. As part of their roots, families need to develop rituals of reconciliation to help members get back in each other's good graces after a blunder. To forgive and to ask for forgiveness is to express caring.

Affection strengthens families by reinforcing the individuals within them. Affection addresses feelings and helps secure bonds between family members by providing a setting for the exchange of feelings and the development of positive self-esteem. When individuals feel accepted and valued, they are free to value and accept others. Affection helps provide that freedom, but love adds another dimension to affection, and that is commitment. It is the difference between being *in love*—as important as that may be—and *loving*. Being in love is a process of give and take. It is feeling good with and about each other. It is meeting each other's needs. It is enhancing each other's happiness. It is, to quote a country song, "love on a good roll." Our culture emphasizes the 'in love' aspect of loving so much that sometimes people become a little confused. They become so tuned in to how that other person is meeting their needs (or not meeting them) that the taking overwhelms the giving. They begin to keep track and tally scores. Sometimes, like Garfield, the cartoon cat who won't share his lasagna until he measures the pieces, they are so worried about getting their share that they apply a mentality of measurement to relationships. Unfortunately, what happens in the process is that love cools just like lasagna does.

Love is give and take, but when the giving always waits on the taking, the loving loses. Love is like a boomerang: you have to throw it out before it can return to you. It is, according to St. Francis of Assisi, *by* giving that we receive and *by* loving that we are loved.

But there are always going to be times when, no matter how well one throws the boomerang, it doesn't come right back. Children, especially, are not always able to return good feelings in kind, and they may be extremely difficult to relate to during certain periods. All relationships undergo transitions and weather difficulties.

When love encompasses commitment as well as affection, the love can continue even when the good feelings are on hold. To paraphrase a popular song that expresses gratitude: "You never gave up on me when I was making things rough on you, and you taught me what love was all about." For parents coping with a stormy period in the life of a child, this song offers the promise that commitment and perseverance can transcend feelings. This same commitment and perseverance is reflected in one of our family's favorite prayers:

Lord, bless our family with openness to real communication, with sharing in all our joys and sorrows, with freedom to let each other grow, with understanding for the gifts each has to give and of course, with love no matter what no matter where. Amen.
Anonymous

4

Control:
Why Parents Teach

This chapter is designed to help parents understand that childhood is a progression along a continuum—from parental control to individual self-control. The roots of self-discipline require parental leadership and a changing balance between protection and preparation, restraint and the wings of relinquishment.

A Changing Balance

Preparation for independence remains one of the primary evolutionary purposes of the family. Each child is expected to progress from an environment in which she experiences good feelings and enjoyable experiences which are primarily controlled by others to one in which she has achieved self-control and is capable of supporting herself and functioning as a competent, independent adult responsive to the needs of others. In the family, movement along this continuum—from dependence to independence, from control to self-control—must be based on confident parental leadership, the communication of clear expectations, the reliability of firm and consistent consequences, and knowledge of the goals of parenting.

Tipping the scales in the direction of parental leadership, involvement, and control does not suggest a return to a repressive authoritarianism that may have characterized past parenting practices. What worked well in an agrarian society where children grew up learning to do exactly what their parents did does not work in our fast-paced, changing world. Those who suggest a revival of old-fashioned authoritarianism may initially succeed in mandating compliance and obedience, especially in pre-adolescents, but they do so at the risk of failing to prepare their children to think, decide, and act independently as competent adults. A solid sense of control is based on a clear knowledge of the purposes of control, and that does not include stifling individuality and freedom of thought. We no longer live in a time in which all parental precepts and knowledge remain accurate and applicable for the next generation. Children need to develop skills in critical thinking, adaptation, and problem-solving—all of which are necessary not only to the successful functioning of a democracy, but perhaps to the very preservation of life on our planet. If children cannot learn these skills in a repressive environment, neither can they in a permissive one. Children are not born responsible; they learn responsibility. Respect for others must be practiced to be perfected, and rights must be exercised in conjunction with accountability. Although parents may strive to raise children who can function competently in a democratic society, they cannot raise them democratically. Children are not created equal to adults in experience, skills, and judgment. Developing that potential is one of the main goals of their growing-up years.

Children need the security of parents who are in charge. They need to know that whoever is in the driver's seat is fully licensed, skilled, and confident. They need the protection of parents who will not give them responsibilities before they have learned to handle them but who will also consistently and cooperatively help them achieve that competence. Children need boundaries, to define not only their physical territory but their behavioral territory as well. J. B. Stockdale reminds us, "Discipline is necessary for freedom; freedom is necessary for excellence."[1] Such an approach to parenting prepares children not only for adulthood but for citizenship as well.

CONTROL GOALS

One of the main differences between faltering and well-functioning families is the quality of leadership that defines parental control. Perhaps the two most important qualities that affect this leadership are intimacy and power. Families work best where power is securely in the parents' hands yet shared "in a complementary rather than a competitive way."[2] What stands out in observations of well-functioning families is that they do not exercise power in heavy-handed ways. Their leadership is an easy leadership because the basic elements of trust and love are present. The parents only rarely appear authoritarian, because children know and understand who is in charge. Although children accept this leadership as appropriate, it is important to remember that all parental decisions are not popular, and that clear goals which the children will grow to understand are behind them. We have identified four common goals of parental control.

GOALS OF PARENTAL CONTROL

1. To reinforce family values and help the child internalize a value system as a guide for behavior.

No one can make decisions in a vacuum. Even the most sophisticated computer needs help making distinctions between *A* and *B* or what is important and what is not. People are no different, and parents need not apologize for expecting behavior that respects family values. In addition, as we emphasized in Chapter 2, shared values are one of the most important contributors to family strength. Parental control should support and reinforce family values.

2. To help the child understand that living in a relationship requires a balance between self-respect and respect for others.

For a preschooler, this may mean taking turns with a friend on the swingset. By the time a child reaches adulthood, parents hope he will have learned to function successfully in a give-and-take fashion that requires him neither to sacrifice his own self-esteem nor to demand it of another person. Parents must insist upon behavior in the family that respects all family members, regardless of age.

3. To learn self-control.

Children come into the world totally focused on their own needs, desires, wishes, and wants. They must learn that there are times to subordinate these to others, to delay gratification, and to (eventually) provide checks on their own behavior. They must learn to express feelings appropriately and to monitor behaviors based upon feelings. Parents must consciously create situations in the home for children to practice self-control.

4. *To prepare for independence and adulthood.*

This responsibility, ideally shared by the home, school, and church, may involve specific skills or general learning—from how to balance a checkbook to creative use of leisure time. It may mean preparation for responsible citizenship or learning consumer skills. It could include becoming comfortable with a computer or competent with a grocery list. In accordance with its own strengths, each home provides opportunities for children to learn the skills they will need as adults.

These control roots—values, respect for self and others, self-control, and self-reliance—can be nurtured by the ways in which parents exercise their leadership, control, and discipline.

HOLDING BACK, LETTING GO

The tug between parents and children for both roots and wings is as natural as the flowing in and out of the tides. At times, parents and children find themselves being pulled in opposite directions as parents seek to balance out the children's need for roots and wings. The very tension which this pull creates is, in and of itself, a healthy, creative one.

When children are small, parents begin by providing freedom within limits and the opportunity to practice new skills with appropriate protection. They take a child who is learning to ride a two-wheeler to the school parking lot, for example, instead of out into the street. Even as the parent assists and encourages, she recognizes that the time comes when she must let go of the bicycle seat and allow the child to learn balance by falling, trying again, and finally riding. The parent cannot prevent either the bruised knee or the bruised ego. Although a parent can identify with the child's feelings of failure, encourage her efforts, and share in her success, it is the child herself who must learn to ride the bike. By building on the successes children experience and helping them profit positively from their failures, parents and children acquire confidence and mutual trust based on reliability.

A model for responsible and cooperative relinquishment becomes so well-established in the family that, by the time the driver of the dirt bike wants the car keys, there should exist an appreciation, on the part of both parents and child, of the demands which (in this example) safety makes on mobility. The child who always went along for the ride is now eager to meet both the legal requirements and parental standards for driving. In her excitement, she may need to be reminded, as firmly and calmly as possible, of the knowledge and skills necessary for safe driving—from parallel parking to reading maps. She may be asked to contribute financially to gasoline bills, or insurance premiums. Most of all, both parent and child must recognize the need to practice with an experienced driver.

Finally, however, the day comes (probably later than the teenager would like and earlier than the parent feels comfortable) to allow the child to drive alone. Relinquishment always carries with it an element not only of trust but also of risk. Roots and wings—we prepare our children as best we know how, but we can't always go with them along the way.

Parents Are Models, Inside-Out

Like other organizations and institutions, families require task organization and accomplishment. In order for a family to run smoothly, certain things need to be done and certain lessons learned. In addition to good feelings and experiences, a family needs structure, discipline, leadership, cooperation, achievement, and accountability. The family is a group for sharing and loving, but it is also a place for learning, and parents are teachers as well as providers and protectors.

Of all the ways that children learn and parents teach, modeling is probably the most important and effective. Everything that parents do is, in a very real sense, model behavior for children. If parents want children to develop self-control and learn self-discipline, they first must look at the models they provide. This applies to how parents control both their inner space—feelings—and their outer space—time and tasks.

Controlling Outer Space

First, parents can help children learn self-discipline by the ways they organize time, tasks, and space in the home. How much organization is enough? The only clear answer to that question is that parents must organize enough to make time for what is important to them as a family. If conversations and shared activities are of high value, then the parents must organize the schedule or household chores to allow time for conversations and shared activities. If entertaining relatives to help solidify family ties is important, then household responsibilities may need to be shared to enable this to take place. If a weekly family night is a priority, then time commitments and the family calendar should be arranged in such a way as to permit this. Sometimes what is required is a shifting of priorities — a sacrificing of some projects in the short run and a relinquishment of others in the long run. At other times, a reordering of present schedules is enough to free up time that previously seemed unavailable.

When is clutter disruptive, and when is it comfortable? The answer to this question varies from person to person. Gary organizes his mind but not his desk, and I can't organize the former until I've straightened up the latter. Because all people are different, the system that works best for a particular family is tailored to that family's specific situation and priorities. The essential prerequisite is an awareness of time as a resource. The organization of space should free up time so that families can spend time in ways that are important to them. Of course, sometimes this cannot be done without a shifting of attitudes or priorities. Some individuals need to give up on the get-it-all-done objective entirely, modify their standards, and let go of their perfectionism. Others must recognize that an abundance of chaos that may not bother them might nevertheless impede the successful functioning of the household. Such individuals need to place a lower value on hanging loose and a higher one on task accomplishment.

For many families, role definitions are in constant transition. The value a couple places on traditional or changing role models, the number of hours worked by each person, and other factors are of far greater importance than trying to meet some external standard that may be more popular in the media than in practice. What works best for any given family is a system that is acceptable to them and that capitalizes, in a complementary fashion, on each person's capacity to contribute. Families should not be dealt with by fractions, but rather by expectations and skills.

The important thing is that parents have a system that enables them to be in control of the household and the chores necessary

to its successful functioning. Some helpful tips along those lines
follow.

FAMILY TIME MANAGEMENT TIPS

Family Activities Schedule. Some kind of master calendar, especially when children reach school age, seems essential to avoid-
ing conflicts, keeping commitments, and safeguarding family
times.

Family Information Center. A centrally located (usually in the
kitchen) family information center is also a definite help,
whether it be a drawer for sports schedules and school menus or
a bulletin board with a family chore chart. The refrigerator (the
most popular appliance in the kitchen) often becomes the place
for posting important family messages.

Individual 'To Do' Lists. Many parents find it helpful to design
separate 'to do' lists according to their roles and responsibilities.
A parent may have a job list, a house list, a family list, a church
list, and a community list. By naming necessary activities and
setting priorities within the categories on each list, a parent can
make the best possible use of the time set aside for each activity.
Within each category, what is of highest importance receives the
first commitment of time and attention. These separate lists enable a person to accomplish by area, poking holes in one's goals
according to the time available.

Find Time for Family Priorities. Family time is frequently overwhelmed by the urgent demands of individual schedules. Strong
families place time together on the calendar and encourage all
family members to plan around these events. No system works
without flaws, which is why Robert Burns's counsel that the
"best laid plans often go astray" is well-taken advice in the family. Household management must be flexible enough to accommodate changes, whether those changes are necessitated by a
sick child or a sudden work assignment. Being well-organized
cannot prevent such unforeseen diversions. It does, however,
give parents a sense of control, of being on top of things—the
assurance that because they are generally well-organized, the
household usually runs smoothly. This knowledge increases
their confidence in coping with those emergencies that do arise.
Effective organization enhances the parents' shared leadership

in the family, and at the same time it serves as a self-discipline model for children who are constantly tuned in to their parents' examples. Although providing a positive model is no guarantee children will embrace a habit, behavior, or value, it powerfully predisposes them to. The ten-year-old who draws up a summer 'To Do' list, the kindergartner who lays out his school clothes the night before, and the high-schooler who designs a study schedule for final exam week are likely applying models learned in the home. The model is what makes the parents' behavioral requirements of their children credible. It is the bridge between who they are as parents and people and what they want their children to become. Parents help children learn the roots of self-discipline by their model of how to organize time, tasks, and space.

CONTROLLING OUR INNER SPACE: FEELINGS

Parents can also help children learn self-discipline by the ways they handle their inner space, their feelings. Children's observations of parents are indiscriminate. They record everything they see and hear, both positive and negative, whether parents are dealing with material realities or internal realities, not only how they do things but how they express their feelings! Children observe, for example, whether parents use anger creatively or to dominate others. They notice when parents attempt to deal with feelings openly and when they use them covertly to manipulate others in order to get their way. These and other models become automatic responses for children as they grow older and find themselves in similar situations. Parental control and discipline, therefore, are strongly assisted or severely compromised by the self-control models parents provide for the expression of feelings and the monitoring of behaviors flowing from those feelings.

It would be futile to advise people not to feel. Feelings are part of the baggage people bring with them as human beings. But how people act upon those feelings, how they display feelings in behavior, and whether they are in control *of* or controlled *by* their feelings are another matter. Yet few of us even acknowledge responsibility for our feelings. Many adults say, 'He made me angry,' or 'She hurt my feelings,' or 'They caused me to feel guilty,' without realizing that in all those situations they are choosing their feelings in accordance with behavior patterns learned a long time ago. In the exact same set of circumstances, therefore, one person will feel hurt, another angry, and a third guilty. To acknowledge to oneself in an emotional situation that 'I'm choosing to feel angry or spiteful or inadequate' can be an important first step in tracking down the sources of feelings and deciding what responses are appropriate to the present situation.

Children learn from models in the home and elsewhere (parents, teachers, neighborhood friends, TV, etc.) which feelings to have in certain situations and how to express those feelings in behavior—whether positive, negative, constructive, or destructive. Children grow up with predispositions to feel and respond in certain ways, and these become almost automatic responses.

Children also learn by trial and error which actions elicit reactions from parents and others that reinforce their feelings. The little girl who likes to surprise Mom by doing the dishes may have learned that the praise she receives contributes to her feeling important and needed. Another child discovers that her teasing of a younger brother brings her more attention (even if negative) than constructive behavior does, and it reinforces her need to be noticed. The feelings parents reinforce in children are negative as well as positive. Because many parents tend to leave children who are being good alone and intervene only when children are misbehaving, some children conclude that negative attention is better than no attention, so they engage in whatever behavior brings them the most attention. A friend shared with us a story about the constant bickering between her two preschool sons. The older child would pick on the younger child until Mother intervened, scolded the older child, and rescued the younger one. One day Mother inadvertently overheard a conversation between the two boys. "Hit me," the younger brother dared. When the older obliged, the younger called out, "Mom, he hit me again!" The two boys were learning a destructive but typical pattern that is a sure winner in its attention-getting value and a loser in its reinforcement of positive feelings and behaviors.

If the affection parents give and the cohesion parents encourage enable families to reinforce positive feelings, the ways in which parents demonstrate emotional self-control help children learn to cope with their inevitable negative feelings. Everybody feels angry, fearful, jealous, guilty, hurt, envious, or inadequate from time to time. Some individuals learn how to put these feelings in perspective; others are dominated by them. Some people, for example, continuously look for opportunities to be angry. An unexpected traffic jam or an innocent remark may be all that is needed to set them off. "That person is always mad," others observe. Another type of person is constantly getting his or her feelings hurt. "She wears her feelings on her sleeve," others say. Some people interpret everything as criticism; they feel defensive and judged. "He takes everything personally," others complain.

Each person tends to have a favorite negative feeling as well as favorite strategies for feeding that feeling. Someone whose favorite negative feeling is anger frequently strikes out, literally or figuratively points the finger, and puts others down. A person whose favorite negative feeling is hurt may sulk. A person whose favorite negative feeling is guilt may use that guilt as a way of manipulating others. Whatever negative feeling becomes the favorite is the product not only of models observed but of attention received. Individuals may become so accustomed to negative feelings that they may actually come to prefer (in a perverse way) feeling angry, hurt, spiteful, or resentful to positive feelings. They resist change because these negative feelings become familiar, elicit predictable responses from others, and require little effort and virtually no risk. Better the certainty of misery than the misery of uncertainty, they conclude. It is easy to see the importance of families tuning in to the feelings they teach and reinforce with their control and approval.

Keeping Touch: Individual Emotion Accounts

If the negative feelings people reveal in behavior aren't challenging enough to understand, there are many other situations in which feelings are hidden at the time they are experienced and then expressed at some later time. This practice has a plausible basis. Certainly a consequence, if not an objective, of parenting is to teach the quality of appropriateness to children. The parenting process itself leads to a host of rules and rhetoric about the appropriate display of feelings. The problem is that, although parents are usually quite adept at letting children know when it is *not* advisable to express emotion ("Use your inside voice," or "You mustn't be angry at your sister," or "You shouldn't act like that"), they do not communicate as effectively when and how it is appropriate to express negative feelings. What most children learn instead is a model for handling feelings that complicates communication and ultimately undermines the self-control it suggests. Some variation of this tendency is an almost universal human characteristic. It is as if people keep mental track of their feelings, like they do their money, in Individual Emotion Accounts (I.E.A.'s).[3]

What children learn by observation is that in situations where it is inappropriate to express negative feelings (talking back to the teacher or a parent), for example, they do not show their emotional reactions at the time. What they do instead is save up these feelings along with the impressive histories behind their accumulation. When this account reaches a certain level, individually determined by observing models, children learn that it is okay to withdraw their saved-up, negative feelings and dump them on someone else. The child learns to feel totally justified at the time. Remorse may come later, but at the time of the dump the child accepts the rationalization that "They had it coming," or "I've put up with this long enough," or "This is the last straw." Both the type of negative feelings saved and the methods of expressing them are learned from models in the home.

This is especially true in the case of anger. Many counselors and psychologists are discovering that being angry, rather than serving to alleviate anger, often entrenches it. In her book, *Anger, the Misunderstood Emotion*,[4] Carol Tavris points out that aggressive behavior actually "escalates anger, solidifies an angry attitude, and establishes a hostile habit." Anger frequently has the opposite effect of catharsis: "Instead of exorcising the anger, it can inflame it." Tavris notes, for example, that when couples yell at each other, "they do not thereafter feel less angry but *more* angry." Tavris counsels that the ventilation of anger is cathartic only when it "restores control and reduces a feeling of powerlessness" so that "why people are angry and what to *do* about it is by far of greater importance than simply ventilating the anger." When parents lose emotional control, they teach children that this is the way to handle feelings, and the save-it-up, dump-it-on cycle is passed on to the next generation. Educators are beginning to notice an increase in youth who come to school so angry at the world that they turn this anger on others indiscriminately. "Children who have lost faith in themselves and others and feel totally rejected resort to revenge-seeking behavior."[5] Likewise, if parents always hold feelings inside and refuse to deal with them at all, they teach children that way of handling feelings.

There are other options, and perhaps the emphasis on restoring control so that parents and children can determine why they are upset and what to do about it is the key to developing emotional self-control. This means giving reason a little time to catch up with feelings so that parents can decide instead of simply reacting.

There are times, of course, when parents will decide that their emotional response is a legitimate and justified reaction to what is happening. Then they must further ask themselves: "What can I do about it?" Sometimes they need to alter the environment, sometimes they need to change their behavior, and sometimes they need to try to influence others to change theirs. It is important to realize that whatever parents do becomes a model of self-control and self-expression for children. When parents show children how to cope with and express negative feelings constructively and how to resolve conflicts, children learn that there are alternatives to saving up feelings and dumping them on others. They learn to separate past feelings from present ones and to recognize that some things simply aren't worth being upset about. Children learn to take charge of their feelings instead of being governed by them. Perhaps they will be guided, as many adults wish to be, by the insight of a prayer that is at once simple and profound:

> Lord, grant me the serenity to accept what I cannot change, the courage to change what I can, and the wisdom to know the difference. Amen.

CONTROL BENEFITS: FOR NOW OR LATER

When parents provide a positive model for emotional self-control in the home, their children have already taken a significant first step in learning self-discipline. As essential as this model is, however, it isn't always sufficient. Children don't grow up exactly like their parents, nor should we expect that. This assumption, that the model will automatically prevail, is wishful thinking on the part of many good parents who fail to exercise proper guidance or adequate controls. Although a good model does often prevail, most children also need to be walked through behaviors to help integrate them. They need to be held accountable to family values and goals, and be allowed to experience appropriate consequences when their behavior violates these codes. Parents need not apologize for teaching children their values, expecting certain behaviors, and discouraging others. This is an integral part of their job description as parents.

Even though parents seek to help their children profit from the best of their knowledge, skills, and experiences, they must remember that children are their own people and not simply clones of themselves. Parents can never reduce child-rearing to a recipe or parenting to a set of prescriptions. The world in which our children will live will not be the same as ours, nor will all parent decisions necessarily be best for children. Gibran reminds us that, although parents can give children their love, they can't superimpose their thinking, for they have their own thoughts, dwelling in the house of tomorrow that parents "visit only in their dreams."[6]

The dreams parents have for their children, then, must be flexible enough so that children have room to fashion their own futures:

> If straight As on a report card is all that will satisfy, then expectations are unreasonable.

> If medicine is the only career choice that will please, then goals are too narrowly defined.

> If a child's SAT score must top 1200 to avoid disappointment, then the expectations have been unfair.

> If tennis must be a child's favorite sport to make the parents happy, the parents are too restrictive.

Parents must seek to equip their children in ways that expand the number of choices they can make that will result in their success, happiness, and sense of contribution. Perhaps this is what family researcher Jerry Lewis meant when he described parental leadership as leaving little doubt who is in charge but still respecting the wants, wishes, and goals of the children.

In a very real sense, parents have two sets of goals for their children—short-term (or immediate) and long-term (or ultimate). But sometimes parents become so overwhelmed with an immediate goal that they lose track of the ultimate objective. Parental control is for both now and later.

In the short run, the goal may be for a child to share his toy; in the long run, parents want him to learn the value of fair play and mutual respect for others. In the short run, parents may want their family to worship together. In the long run, they hope that the children will internalize a value system that recognizes the importance of religious commitment and community. In the short run, the goal may be for a child do her homework before she watches TV. In the long run, her parents want her to develop self-discipline habits which will help her in meeting her responsibilities as well as cultivating leisure-time activities. In the short run with children, parents are often content with compliance, but in the long run, they want self-motivation.

Immediate and ultimate goals are both important to effective parental control, discipline, and leadership. Parents do not want to lose sight of their long-term control objectives—an internalized value system, reciprocal respect, self-control, and preparation for independence. They must realize, however, that these goals are achieved on a day-by-day basis in a thousand different situations in which they guide their children through the specific behaviors necessary to support the goals. They do this by using a wide range of discipline approaches which protect, prepare, and teach.

Some control strategies are primarily targeted at securing conformity. They are likely to result in compliance, willing or unwilling, and may or may not encourage self-control. For example:

> a two-year-old running toward a busy street may receive a swift smack on her padded behind. We want her to stay away from the street, and if fear of punishment is the motive, so be it.

> A boisterous child interrupting a conversation for the third time is reprimanded. We want him to learn to wait politely, and his awareness of reciprocal respect is only secondarily a motive.

> A teenager is grounded for a weekend for coming home an hour after curfew. Her parents want her to be on time or to call if there is a reason she can't.

Other control strategies encourage self-responsibility directly:

A sixth-grader comes home from school with an hour's worth of homework to do. A friend calls and asks him to play. The parents let him decide, explaining that there will be no TV after supper until the homework is done. The child decides.

Parents have recurrent problems regarding the showering habits of their three teenagers. Complaints range from poor clean-up afterward to using up all the hot water. They ask the children to develop some rules for the shower to which they can all agree.

An eighteen-year-old wants to buy a used car. His parents review his financial obligations with him, and he gets a part-time job in order to meet them.

Both kinds of strategies—those targeted primarily at compliance and conformity, and those more likely to encourage self-responsibility—are necessary and can be effective in discipline. Both kinds can be useful throughout childhood. It stands to reason, however, that the older and more mature children become, the more opportunities they should be given to learn and practice self-discipline. We want to help them move along a continuum

- from parental control to self-control.
- from self-centeredness to respect for others.
- from external to internal motivation.
- from imposed values to internalized and authenticated ones.
- from dependence to independence and, ultimately, to interdependence.
- from roots to wings.

THE CONTROL CONTINUUM

There are many books on disciplining children. Some simply dispense advice, and others propose intricate systems into which the parent plugs every situation. Without denigrating the value of various approaches, no book or system (this one included)

```
X-----------------------------------------------------------------X
Parent                                                      Child
Centered                                                  Centered
Cruise Control    Conscious Control    Dual Control    Self-Controled
```

can anticipate or address all the questions and concerns parents will have about disciplining their children. It is not possible to provide answers to all questions or solutions to all problems. Each child is different, each parent is different, and so is each family. Values differ and so does what parents consider acceptable behavior for children or effective disciplines to use. While some discipline strategies are compatible with a family's style of parenting, others may seem unrealistic or unworkable, too hard or too soft. A strategy that worked well with a friend's child may fall flat when applied to another family. Furthermore, the problems families face—even if similar in nature—may require dramatically different approaches depending upon the environments in which they live.

We do not want, therefore, to simply suggest a list of recommended strategies. What we do hope to do is make parents more aware of what they hope to accomplish with their discipline and how they are using their control to help encourage their children's progression along the continuum toward self-control. Only thus can parents appreciate the central role control occupies in parenting—to help protect and prepare children as parents guide them on their journeys toward adulthood. The strategies selected here were chosen because they help illustrate steps along the way. They are not meant to be either inclusive or definitive. Parents will immediately begin to relate other models to this way of thinking about discipline and add strategies that have worked well for them. Whether a specific strategy is effective for any given family depends upon many factors—even their definition of success.

There are many times, of course, when a child's compliance is a more important objective than his learning self-discipline. It would be preposterous, for example, for a parent to knowingly allow a teenager to discover the consequences of experimenting with drugs. On the other hand, even small children can be self-responsible in certain areas of their lives—selecting which play clothes to wear, for example.

Although for any given child movement along the control

continuum is generally in a forward direction (from dependence to independence, from control to self-control), this does not mean that a child moves ahead in all aspects of his life concurrently or at a steady pace. Nor does it mean that all children's timetables for growth and independence are identical. Some children are more mature intellectually than emotionally, or vice-versa. Some young children's physical coordination far outdistances their attention span, or vice-versa. Some children are more task-mature than others. Children sometimes grow in leaps and bounds and at other times experience lapses. Certain growth and development (for adults as well as children) requires a settling-in time, a status-quo stopover for reflection and integration. Control strategies must reflect these differences. Knowing when to restrain and when to relinquish, when to nudge and when to wait, when to be strong and when to be gentle requires a sensitivity that is learned not only with the mind but also with the heart—sometimes through success, sometimes through failure. Parenting is more than a set of skills and strategies. It is more an art than a science. It requires intuition as well as intellect, forgiveness as well as firmness, wisdom as well as love.

Let us again use the analogy of learning to drive a car (a familiar one in almost all families), this time applying it to parental discipline. One can see how certain control strategies are more likely to encourage compliance and others encourage independence. One can even spot the techniques that are less likely to be effective at encouraging either.

Sometimes parents relate to children almost automatically, as if driving on a deserted interstate with the car set on *cruise control*. There are no stoplights and very little traffic. With a little luck, they will be able to maintain a constant speed, listen to a tape, and even daydream a little en route to their destination. Just as one pushes a button to switch on a car's cruise control, so parents frequently respond predictably and automatically with a minimum of mental effort to things their children do or say. It's almost as if the children have pushed a button and the parents have switched into cruise control parenting.

Of course, it is not only children whom parents respond to in this fashion. All human beings are preprogrammed with automatic responses to fit certain situations. When one person asks, "How are you?" another responds without even thinking,

"Fine, and how are you?" They have simply engaged the greeting ritual button. Such buttons save both time and energy by enabling people to respond in countless situations with minimal effort. Because cruise control responses are based on the past (how one learned to handle similar situations a long time ago), they may or may not work well in the present. Some people's automatic responses serve them more effectively than others' do. An objective of counseling is to help troubled individuals re-examine inappropriate reactions and learn new ones, but everyone can certainly profit from periodic re-examination of these button responses.

There may be stretches of deserted interstate in child-rearing or trouble-free times when parents can relate to and discipline children almost automatically. Most people can point to at least one example of highly successful parents who seem to combine just the right amounts of fairness, firmness, and love to bring their children into adulthood almost automatically, but such parents are rare indeed. Although parents can be grateful for trouble-free times, they must still stay alert for changes in the weather, an increase in traffic, or unanticipated dangers.

They must be ready to shift gears if necessary and take *conscious control*. The parent is still in the driver's seat but now consciously decides—based on family values, behavioral consequences, the needs of the children, and the objectives of discipline—which discipline strategies to use. These conscious control strategies are not automatic; they are thoughtful, considered, and considerate. Designed primarily to secure compliance, these strategies may also encourage self-discipline.

Dual control strategies should be used in situations where a child is ready to share responsibility. Like the special cars equipped for driver education classes, these strategies allow practice with protection, permitting the child to develop the skills, competence, and confidence that are prerequisites to self-discipline.

Finally comes *self-control*, when a child is both ready and responsible. The home base is still at the end of each solo flight, and parents are still available for consultation and encouragement as a child masters new skills. Let us now examine some of the specific control strategies in these categories.

Cruise Continuum

	Cruise Control	Conscious Control	Dual Control	Self-Control
Roots Parent Approach	Automatic Behavior	Thoughtful Strategies	Shared Responsibility Mutual Accountability	Protected Independence
			— WING PLANS-----	
Wings Child Response	Compliance	Compliance	Practiced Independence	Self-Discipline

Ultimate Goal—to protect and prepare
Present Objective—to encourage compliance or independence

Cruise Control (It's Automatic)

As suggested earlier, cruise control parenting does not adapt well to changing conditions. In the areas of affection, cohesion, and perhaps even affiliation—where good models exist for the display of nurturing, sharing, and relating—it is probably easier to rely on what was learned in the past than it is in discipline, leadership, and control, areas which are often problem-based. The need to be loved and belong doesn't change. But the problems, dangers, and difficulties families encounter often do, and so must the strategies available to handle them. It is easier, therefore, to identify the pitfalls of cruise control parenting in the areas of control and discipline than it is in the other three areas. There already exists a set of collective cruise control strategies which, if not socially sanctioned, are at least generally understood, easily recognized, and readily identified as typical parent responses. This list probably contains examples of techniques that most parents rely on at one time or another to get the job done. They are also likely to appear on lists of things one said one would never do or say as parents. It seems almost inevitable that comments like 'Because I told you so' will eventually slip the lips of most parents, either to re-establish authority or out of frustration or fatigue.

These strategies may or may not result in compliance in the short run, but they are unlikely to do so in the long run. Often they reinforce a child's diminished self-image, and they do little to teach self-discipline. We list them here not because parents won't use them from time to time but because they will. Parents need to recognize the limitations of these strategies and begin to substitute alternative ones that are more likely to result in either compliance, self-discipline, or both.

Negative Cruise Control

Name Calling. Here names are used to invoke shame or guilt.

> "There you go again acting like a baby."
>
> "How can you be so lazy/stupid/thoughtless?"
>
> "Can't you ever get anything right?"

Even if a child can escape the negative self-image such comments reinforce, she is not likely to pay much attention to such disparaging comments as motives for changing her behavior as she grows older.

Threats. Threats are thrown like darts in hopes of coercing behavior through fear rather than follow-up.

> "If you don't stop teasing Roger right this moment, you can go to your room and forget about going to Mike's birthday party."
>
> "Stop that immediately or you'll get what's coming to you."
>
> "If you aren't back in time for supper, you'll regret it, believe me."

Frequently when parents threaten, they later decide that the threatened action is too stern for the behavior. Then they are faced with compromising their credibility by not following up on the threat, or compromising their judgment by doing so. Perhaps that is why it brings a smile when we hear Claire Huxtable of "The Cosby Show" threaten, "I don't want anyone in this house to touch anyone again for any reason for the rest of their lives."

Comparing to Others. Just as adults want to be appreciated for who they are instead of judged for who they are not, so children tend to resent comments that compare them negatively to others as the inspiration for improvement. Such comments are more likely to encourage rebellion or despair than improvement.

"I wish you did as well in school as your brother."

"Why can't you come home and get your homework done immediately like your sister does?"

"You are a smart alec, just like your Uncle Rodney."

Running It Into the Ground. We don't know how to resolve the dilemma between saying what we say so often that the children grow sick of hearing it and saying it often enough that it registers. Balance is definitely required—probably too much for the children's liking and too little for the parents' comfort. If you have a solution to this one, let us know.

'You Tell' Messages. These are a shorthand way of communicating which parents sometimes use to save time or avoid delivering unpleasant messages themselves.

"Dear, you tell Jerome that if he doesn't finish his homework, he can't watch TV."

"Lakia, you tell your brother that if he is late for dinner one more time, he is doing the dishes."

And of course, brother slips in at the table with perfect timing right before the family joins hands for table grace. He is smug, and Lakia—whose night it was to do dishes anyway—is denied yet another reprieve by a matter of mere seconds.

Guilt Trips. It isn't hard to imagine, even as parents find themselves saying the words, the limited impact of: "After all I've done for you, why can't you take out the trash without complaining?" Constantly appealing to children's sense of guilt is counterproductive to their developing internal motivation, despite how justified the comment may seem to the parent.

Do What I Say, Not What I Do. Parents often communicate this message even when they don't actually say the words. Of course, children skim right over the first part of the sentence because what parents *do* truly speaks more loudly than what they *say.* Research confirms, in sometimes frightening ways, how often children simply play back or repeat models learned at home. The majority of child abusers, for example, grew up in homes in which they were abused. Adolescent girls who become pregnant are often the children of mothers who bore babies in their teen years. One of the most discouraging aspects of social work, psychology, and counseling is the realization that it is difficult to break negative cycles of behavior from one generation to the next.

There are many other examples of negative cruise control parenting. What is important is not that parents find themselves using some of these responses but to be able to recognize them. In addition, parents must realize that, in the long run, negative cruise control will reap resentment and/or rebellion. Re-assessment is essential.

Positive Cruise Control

Obviously not all of our automatic responses are negative. There is such a thing as positive cruise control as well. Just as many parents hold and caress a new baby automatically (affection), do things together (cohesion), or relate to close relatives and friends (affiliation) without having to stop and think about it, so parents may also employ constructive control and discipline automatically.

CONSCIOUS CONTROL (SHIFTING GEARS)

This process of thoughtful re-examination leads us to the second set of strategies along the control continuum—*conscious control*. Here parents take the car out of cruise control. They shift gears as it is appropriate to the smooth operation of the vehicle and road conditions. The decisions they make are not always popular with the children in the back seat ("You have to wear your seat belts"), but they are made in conscious consideration of the family's values and the needs, wishes, and wants of the children. The parents are in charge. They share the power, not heavy-handedly but as a matter of course.

Into this category fall those strategies which many parents have found useful in securing compliance but which may or may not encourage self-discipline any more than explaining traffic laws teaches children how to drive. Learning, listening, and complying, however, are prerequisites to the skill-building needed for self-discipline.

Performance-Based Praise and Criticism

When parents want to reinforce children's positive behaviors or call attention to their negative ones, it is more effective to focus on specific actions than it is to use character adulations or character indictments. General, sweeping statements of praise such as "Oh, you're an angel" or "You're Mama's good boy" are not as effective at reinforcing a specific behavior as are more direct, to-the-point statements such as, "I really appreciated your emptying the dishwasher," or "Thanks for taking out the trash." These latter comments help a child understand specifically which behavior has pleased, and they don't confuse parental acceptance and love with doing certain deeds. (Of course, parents are giving the child lots of affection and unconditional acceptance in situations not related to his doing specific deeds.) It is important that parents look harder for actions to praise in their children than those to correct. Some psychologists have even suggested that parents should find twice as much in their children's behavior to reinforce as they do to disparage. One child psychologist says we need to "catch them being good."

Similarly, negative comments are easier for a child to accept when they refer to a single, specific behavior rather than becoming a reason for indicting the personality or character of the child. That could mean the difference between a parent saying, "There you go again, being a big bully," and saying, "It's Michael's turn to choose the game because you did last time." We were amused one time to hear our daughter unconsciously apply this principle in practice, if not in spirit, when she reprimanded one of her brothers with the comment, "That was a jerky thing to do."

Discounts

Discounts are probably one of the most attractive and yet most difficult to apply of the conscious control strategies. To discount—give no attention at all—to negative behavior can be effective when a child's behavior is primarily motivated by its attention-getting value. A discount's effectiveness rests on the recognition that there is a strong tendency for children to behave in whatever ways bring them the most attention, negative or positive. Ideally, if parents can discount (ignore) negative attention-getting behaviors, they eliminate the motivation for engaging in them. This works especially well when parents are at the same time doubling up on the attention a child receives for positive behaviors.

Discounts can be useful strategies, but like right turns on red, they must be used with caution. Parents cannot discount behavior which risks bodily harm or destruction of property, for example. Neither will a discount work well when the behavior is being reinforced in another context. Few younger brothers and sisters, for example, will ignore an older sibling's teasing, and their reactions are more than enough to fuel the attention-getting behavior. Nor will parental discount of a adolescent's negative behavior be effective when that same behavior is being recognized and reinforced by the peer group.

A discount *can* sometimes be effective as a means of coping with some of the emotional flip-flops of adolescence, however. Although no parent has to tolerate rudeness or disrespect, parents must appreciate the very real need adolescents have to test limits—if not in actions, at least in arguments. Comments are frequently stated in the most extreme fashion, and parents, predictably, react in kind. If parents can withhold their own emotional reactions, they can often function as sounding boards for their children.

What parents need to remember is that what is important is what they want to accomplish with their discipline, not just what they want to communicate. The object is not to make points but to help young people learn how to think decisions through, weigh pros and cons, and anticipate consequences.

Follow-Through

When Gary was in elementary school, he was once graded on attentiveness. We may smile at the thought of young children trying to meet this expectation, but it has occurred to us that attentiveness is one area in which parents often perform poorly. Many parents today simply do not pay enough attention to discipline. They don't follow through.

If a family's rules, procedures, and systems are so important to its competent functioning, the first question one might ask is: Are there such rules and procedures in operation in the home? Are they clearly articulated and understood by the children? Is there opportunity, as the children grow older, for them to help shape these rules and expectations? Do the parents follow through? Are they attentive? 'The buck stops here' is a truism in parenting as well as political leadership. It may be the child's job to feed the dog, but the parent must be sure that this chore is accomplished in a timely fashion (if not for the sake of the child, for the sake of the dog). If the child is supposed to clean his room and forgets to do so, the parent must follow through with the agreed-upon consequence. When parents continually rescue children from their responsibilities—emptying the trash for them when they forget, repeatedly taking the homework left on the dining room table to school, or overlooking consequences for unacceptable behavior—children come to depend upon their parents to be responsible for them. They don't assume ownership of their own activities and behaviors. There is obviously an element of grace here, and expectations must be appropriate. A parent is not doing a child a favor by consistently robbing him or her of opportunities to be responsible. Follow-through is probably one of the most neglected aspects of parenting today. Too many parents do not possess enough time, energy, and determination to hang in there and make sure the job gets done. They conclude that it's just not worth the hassle, and the child quickly learns just how much hassle is necessary to help them reach that conclusion. Conscious control requires consistent attention and committed follow-through.

Rewards

Many parents, eager to avoid the negative aspects of punishment, prefer to reward children for good behavior rather than punish them for its opposite. There is a popular plausibility to this approach. That children (and adults, too) tend to repeat behaviors which are positively reinforced is a well-accepted psychological principle. Tangible rewards can work well, especially in situations where the behavior being acknowledged is habitual or rote. Toilet-training successes may be recognized with balloons or candy. A new toy may be offered as incentive for giving up a ratty blanket. Tangible rewards often work well in situations where a child has yet to achieve the maturity or motivation to strive for the desired behavior without some incentive, or in situations where the short-term benefits outweigh any long-term difficulties. Parents may buy silence at a wedding, for example, with the promise of a chocolate sundae afterward. We recall an unqualified success with one of our children by offering Hershey's Krackel bars for mastering the multiplication tables.

Proponents of the raise-them-by-reward school of thought point to the success of certain programs for troubled youths that reward progress with points which can then be converted into privileges. Rewards can work, but there are qualifications and consequences. For example, programs that seem to work well with troubled teens may reward acceptable behavior with privilege points, but they usually also provide for a loss of points when behavior violates the codes. Although many people would like to discipline children only positively, such an approach is unrealistic for parents as well as for children. It is appropriate for parents to strive to go out their our way to recognize positive behaviors (even at a ratio of two to one). Parents may try to 'catch their children being good,' but parents are still left with the necessity of also addressing unacceptable behaviors. So what role can rewards play in control and discipline?

Use Tangible Rewards Sparingly. When a parent's primary approach to discipline is offering rewards for good behavior, what are the dangers? First of all, the need escalates. A child who is promised a new toy for going to bed without a fuss one night soon requires that same reward every night. A forty-nine-cent favor might work the first time, but that more-expensive toy advertised on TV may be needed to do the trick on subsequent occasions. If it takes a toy to motivate a six-year-old to good behavior, will it take a car once he is sixteen?

Of even greater significance is that a material reward system compromises one of the parent's major behavioral objectives—teaching self-motivation. The child begins to perceive the activity for which the reward is offered as one that, in and of itself, is probably of little value. It may be the difference between a teacher promising first-graders: "You can all play this math game if you will do your reading first." Or: "You may read a story if you will do this math game first." Understandably, in each case the class will tend to interpret the latter activity as a drudge and the former as a prize. What parents (and teachers) ultimately want from children is internal, not external, motivation. To offer rewards for all good behavior is to rob children of the opportunity to experience the value of an activity separate from its reward.

Finally, the less dependent people are on others to meet their survival needs, the less motivated they are to work for a reward system anyway. When physical needs such as safety and survival are at stake, people are highly motivated to repeat those behaviors which are reinforced and avoid those which are discouraged. That same motivation is not always present when survival is not at stake.

Use Intangible Rewards Wisely. Don't parents also reward children's behavior by praising them? The answer, of course, is yes. Positive attention and praise are also powerful motivators. Two distinctions need to be made, however. First, when it comes to control and discipline, parents do not want to confuse their love with their children's conformity. The child, therefore, must be praised in terms of the specific behavior they want to reinforce, not because that behavior is a condition for parental affection. For example, a parent may say to a seven-year-old, "Thanks for cleaning your room—it looks great," instead of "Pick up all your toys and then I'll give you a big hug." Unequivocal, unconditional statements ("I love you," "You're a doll") are better said in other contexts as expressions of our undiluted affection rather than as rewards for good behavior.

Second, whenever possible, praise should reinforce the child's accomplishment and sense of satisfaction and not simply the parent's pleasure in it. ('Wow! That play worked perfectly. You must have been pleased.') This reinforces the good feeling the child receives for success and accomplishment. "I was so proud when you made that touchdown" focuses on the *parent's* reaction and communicates to the child the concern that Mom and Dad might not be proud when he fumbles the ball in the future.

The student who receives a good grade on a report on which she worked long and hard might be acknowledged with 'I'll bet all that work seems worthwhile now,' rather than 'You're so smart. Aren't we lucky to have such a bright girl?'

Rewards, tangible and intangible, are important tools for control and discipline. They are not the only tools needed and certainly will not work in every situation, but they can be helpful when used appropriately.

Punishments

Punishment also has a place in parental control. Although subject to abuse, misuse, overuse, and underuse, punishment can be effective in reinforcing compliance, demonstrating parental credibility, and teaching behavioral consequences. However, parents must be willing to act and not just react, to be purposeful and not simply powerful. Although they may feel angry, the reason they punish a child is not to find an outlet for their anger but to teach a lesson not being learned in more positive ways. Although it is unreasonable to expect that children will *like* being punished, they can appreciate the justice of their parents' punishments if those punishments are consistent, specific, immediate, and proportional.

Consistent punishment comes as no surprise to children. It is in response to clearly articulated, well-understood, and generally accepted standards of behavior in the home. If the consequence of leaving a bed unmade is docking the child twenty-five cents on next week's allowance, the child who leaves a bed unmade will expect that punishment.

Specific punishment targets a single unacceptable behavior and not a whole host of negative character traits. For example, 'You may not use the car for a week because you did not bring it home at the agreed-upon time' is not the same as 'When will you ever learn to be considerate of others? No car privileges for being such a thoughtless clod.'

Immediate punishment emphasizes the importance (especially with young children) of following the unacceptable behavior with the punishment soon enough for the child to make the connection. 'Because you did not stay in the yard this morning, you must stay inside the rest of the day' is more effective than, 'This weekend you can have no friends over because you left the yard this morning.'

Finally, the punishment should be *proportional* to the deed. Our children taught us this when we devised an elaborate system to motivate them to keep their rooms clean which resulted in loss of part of their allowance: "Don't dock for a sock," they counseled us. The key to choosing the punishment is to start with the least restrictive way of making the necessary point and teaching the needed lesson. Parents need to leave ample room to escalate, if necessary. It goes without saying that some situations, especially where the potential for serious harm exists (drug and alcohol abuse, for example, or careless driving), that the punishment must be restrictive enough to decisively discourage repetition of the behavior. Other avenues of influence (such as counseling, group sessions, and so on) may also need to be explored in such situations.

Because punishments are almost always seen as negative by children, they have the potential to produce negative side effects — resentment, anger, and rebellion. This is to be expected and accepted. On the other hand, in other contexts parents should go out of their way to find positive behaviors they can reinforce in their children. They should also continue to offer support, love, and affection. With this reservoir of good will parents help children learn self-control and adhere to family behavioral standards.

Among the punishments parents have found effective are: (1) *spanking*, (2) *reprimands*, (3) *separation* or *isolation*, (4) *groundings*, and (5) *loss of privileges*. Again, it is appropriate when selecting a punishment to keep the consistent, specific, immediate, and proportional criteria in mind. Other important factors to consider include the age, maturity, and likely response of the child. The specific situation and the range of strategies already tried will also influence the choice of punishment.

Spankings, for example, quickly become ineffective when they are overused and as a child grows older. A smack on the behind is primarily useful (if at all) when a child is too young to reason and in situations that involve health and safety. Some parents have also found spankings effective at times when a child is determined to test the limits or is totally unresponsive to reason. But spankings are short-term strategies targeted at compliance alone. When a parent relies on physical punishment as a primary disciplinary strategy for young children, or as a continuing one as a child grows older, that parent needs to immediately search for and identify other options. Ultimately, parents cannot teach self-control by force and through fear, even when that force is employed with the utmost restraint.

A *reprimand* may be an effective punishment in some instances. Depending upon the child (some children shape up when parents look at them cross-eyed), a stern 'That is enough — you will stop teasing Roger immediately' may result in quick compliance, which is the sole objective of this strategy.

Much of the socialization process for children is the result of the ways in which they tune in to the likes and dislikes of their parents, whether stated verbally or nonverbally. A reprimand serves as a notice that the child is not meeting behavioral expectations, and it is often adequate to influence a change in behavior. When this is not the case, however, parents who use reprimands must be prepared to follow up with alternative strategies.

Separation (or *isolation*) has several variations. A parent may decide, for example, to send a misbehaving child to his room for a time-out. The old standing in the corner strategy practiced by the parents of *Dennis the Menace* is an example of this technique. For active children, being still for even a short time may be an effective punishment. A parent may also use this approach to separate two children who are bickering, thus removing them from each other and the source of irritation: 'Since you cannot play that game without fighting, each of you will find something else to play alone for the next half hour.' Or the parent may decide to retreat from the situation: 'I feel angry at both of you right now; I am going to read my book without interruption for ten minutes, and then we will talk about this problem.' These options alter the environment in which the problem occurs. Although compliance is an objective, these strategies have the added advantage of teaching the parties involved to use time to control emotional responses and make way for more reasoned reactions.

When punishment precedes unfinished business in the parent-child relationship, parents must remember to get back to the problem at hand. An opportunity for problem-solving and discussion is then present. Dialogue such as 'How can we handle a problem like this one in the future so that we don't all end up angry?' can be productive.

Groundings and *loss of privileges* become useful strategies as children grow older and can comprehend the consequences of behavior. These punishments demonstrate that freedom and responsibility go hand-in-hand and have the potential for teaching self-responsibility as well as encouraging compliance. The more clearly parents are able to demonstrate the connection between a punishment and a child's behavior, the more effective that punishment is likely to be. To the extent that parents do this, they increase the likelihood of affecting long-term self-discipline as well as short-term compliance:

Because I did not study and my grades have suffered, I am
not allowed to watch TV on school nights this grading period.

Because I did not call and say I would be late, I do not get
to use the car the rest of the week.

Because I did not do my chores, my allowance will be
docked.

Because I telephoned my out-of-town friend without permission, I will pay the long distance charge.

Because my friend and I bought some cigarettes and tried
smoking on the bike trail, I am grounded for two weeks.

Some psychologists refer to punishments such as these as 'logical consequences' because there seems to be a logical connection between the behavior and the consequence. The logic behind the consequence is often clearer to the parent than to the
child, and although identifying it may be an admirable objective
for parents, it will probably be perceived by the child as punishment nevertheless.

Institutions for troubled youngsters often develop point systems that demonstrate a clear relationship between acceptable
and unacceptable behaviors and plus and minus points which
are, in turn, connected with privileges or a loss of privileges.
Such structured, unambiguous systems have also been found to
be effective in families whose children have serious problems —
drug and alcohol abuse, for example, or running away. One approach to control and discipline that involves a national network of parent groups is called Tough Love. It has helped many
parents communicate both their expectations and behavioral
consequences clearly. Sometimes this results in painful consequences such as not allowing a child to come home until he or
she is willing to live by the rules of the house — rules that forbid
alcohol and drugs, for example. Such difficult decisions are best
made in the supportive atmosphere of a group like Tough Love.

Some parents we know have found modified point systems to
be useful in ordinary family situations involving less serious
problems but ones which nevertheless seem to resist resolution.
One such example is a parent who puts a toy away for a set period of time after the child has accumulated a certain number of
points for leaving the toy lying on the living room floor. Obvi-

ously, the child must by old enough to appreciate the relationship between the behavior and the consequence. (One can't help but wonder what the consequences would be of so confiscating a teenager's athletic shoes.)

Another technique that is sometimes effective with older children is to tally points for put-downs or—as they have come to be called in our family—unnecessary negative comments. The child who accumulates a certain number of points within a week may be asked to do something especially thoughtful or helpful for the family.

DUAL CONTROL TO SELF-CONTROL

Finally, there are control strategies that teach and encourage independence and self-discipline. These strategies fall along the control continuum somewhere between dual control and self-control. They require of parents relinquishment as well as participation, practice as well as preparation, permission as well as protection, support as well as accountability. In the case of dual control strategies, parents share responsibility with their children; self-control strategies require that parents relinquish responsibility to their children.

Show and Tell is Not Enough

Tell me, I hear.
Show me, I see.
Involve me, I learn.

The validity of this Chinese proverb is acknowledged by most educators. Children learn best when parents teach them not only by words and actions but by allowing them to participate in the process, too. This approach can be effective in teaching character content as well as subject matter. Parents can not only explain to a child what behaviors are appropriate and why, but they can also show the child how to act and then give the child the opportunity to practice. This approach can be used right on the scene, as in the case of a small child who has silently accepted a cookie from a neighbor by reminding, "What do we say when Mrs. Collins offers us a treat?" Or they may talk about such situations at another time and practice appropriate responses together. For example:

PARENT: What do we say when somebody gives us a treat?

CHILD: Thank you. I really like chocolate chip cookies.

With older children, too, it is sometimes helpful to anticipate situations in which they might confront values decisions and discuss various options. Our children had a church-school teacher at the junior-high level who presented them with the opportunity to role-play values choices. They not only discussed faith perspectives on typical temptations teens face, but they had the opportunity as well to practice strategies in advance to help them face problems. In some situations, they practiced comfortable ways of saying no. The idea behind the lesson, of course, was that having an acceptable response prepared in advance would prevent them from impulsively going along with behaviors simply because they could not think fast enough on the spot. Parents must tell as well as show. And finally, they must involve children if children are to learn for themselves.

Check In Instead of Check Up

In homes where accountability has been treated like a one-way street, what often evolves by the time children reach their mid-teens is a contest in which the parents, like cops, feels compelled to check up on their children. Adolescents, who often define freedom as the absence of accountability, want to own their own time, actions, and schedule. They volunteer little about what exactly this means, and the parent is left with cross-examination to fill in the details. This describes the inevitable generation gap; children often push for freedom before their parents are willing to give it. There is an expectation, however, that parents can begin developing early, an approach that promotes resolution of accountability conflicts and can be especially helpful in working out accommodations with older teens and young-adult children who still live at home. This approach recognizes the importance of mutual respect and consideration. Accountability is a two-way street.

Parents who hope to achieve this rapport need to communicate, in both words and actions, this mutual dependence in the family. For example, parents who tell their children where they are going and when they will return, or call when they are late, demonstrate reliability which makes meaningful the requirement that the children do so also. Checking in becomes, therefore, an act of mutual consideration, not a contest of wills with the child maintaining that such reporting is an affront to his independence. By the parent's example and expectations, the child recognizes the responsibilities of living in a family. The reliability of mutual regard is one way to build trust in families.

Natural Consequences

This is another useful strategy designed to transfer ownership from the parent to the child. It is distinguished from the logical consequences strategy mentioned earlier because the consequence is not simply selected by the parent and possibly perceived by the child as arbitrary or unrelated to the action; rather, it flows directly from the behavior. This is life teaching about life. Certainly, there are natural consequences which parents cannot permit their children to experience. Where health and safety are concerned, for example, parents must intervene. These are areas where the parent protects rather than permits the child to live by the consequence.

A few years ago, psychologists were advising parents to allow children to take complete responsibility for their homework. School, they pointed out, was the child's domain, not the parents' problem. This sounded all too attractive to parents coping with the demands of dual careers. What happened, of course, is that many children simply did not accept ownership. They had not yet learned to value hard work and responsibility, nor were they mature enough to appreciate the consequence of taking the easy way out and watching TV instead of doing math. This backing-off of parental support and follow-up continues to contribute to the crisis in our schools. Parents are now being urged to become more involved in their children's schooling, to share the responsibility with teachers and become partners in the education of their children. Obviously, some children require more shepherding than others. This caution aside, there *are* times when parents can allow children to experience the natural consequences of their behavior and learn directly from the experience:

The child who spends his allowance at the beginning of the

week on candy and soft drinks doesn't have enough money
to see a movie on Saturday.

The teenager who forgets to put his favorite shirt in the
wash doesn't have it available to wear for the Friday night
dance unless he washes it himself.

The student who doesn't allow enough time for a science
project stays up all night completing it.

Allowing children to learn from experience is, for many parents, one of the most difficult strategies to apply. It is a dual control strategy because it depends on parental restraint. What it
requires of parents is not talk and action but silence and non-
intervention. Parents must neither chastise nor rescue, and they
must resist the temptation to cap the consequence with an 'I told
you so.'

Developing Wings

The final self-control strategy we want to discuss is called developing wing plans. Parents need to identify specific areas in
which children, at appropriate ages, can gradually assume ownership and responsibility and thus begin to develop wings. Examples of such areas include: dating, use of the car, household
chores, curfews, schedules, homework, wardrobe, hair styles,
money, and TV or VCR viewing.

Sometimes it is helpful for parents to select specific ages at
which certain responsibilities will become the child's. At other
times, an assessment of the child's readiness is more important
than an arbitrary age. What's important is that parents give
freedom and responsibility in synchronization with each other,
gradually, and that they be age-appropriate. Many people believe that parents today give children too many choices too early
and thus create confusion, insecurity, or a misplaced precocious-
ness. A young mother we knew developed the habit of consulting with her two- and four-year-old about what they wanted for
lunch until she discovered that she was preparing two different
menus each day. How much more appropriate for the parent to
simply make the decision, prepare the meal, and announce that
lunch is ready.

Wardrobe and Hairstyle. Two areas in which children are likely
to covet ownership are what they wear and how they style their

hair. Both of these areas can be used to help a child develop wings. Examples of wardrobe wings plans would be allowing a five-year-old to select play clothes from a special drawer or an elementary-age child to choose school clothes the night before. In the latter case, Mom or Dad is available to consult on color coordination or appropriateness. The parent can begin to teach smart shopping by taking the school-age child along to buy clothes, helping him learn to compare prices and judge quality. The junior-high student might do some shopping on her own or with friends and even spend some of her own money that she earned babysitting. By high school, shopping trips can be social events, times for a parent and a child to simply be together as well as to make needed purchases. The parent continues to counsel and set limits, but the final decision, within these parameters, is the child's. Sometimes it will take more than one trip to the mall to find an article of clothing that satisfies both the parents' price and practicality requirements and the child's style specifications. We recall our daughter informing Gary when she was in junior high that she did not want "a coat that looked durable." By the time a shopper is a senior in high school, she may be buying many of her own clothes, perhaps with a clothing allowance supplemented by extra money she earns at a part-time job. This illustrates one possible wing plan in this area. Keep in mind, however, that flight plans need to be not only age-appropriate but also adapted to the particular child. For example, there was nothing our two sons liked doing less than going shopping. It wasn't until they got to high school that they wanted to replace the old system of us simply ordering what they needed out of a catalog.

As for how children wear their hair, parents are on their own! We decided that this decision belonged to the children as soon as they were able to handle a blow dryer competently, a skill usually not acquired before seventh grade. But the most radical hairstyle to which we were subjected was a modified spike for one summer season, so we may not be the most experienced sources in this area. Adolescents do seem to have a real need to identify with the peer group in dress and hairstyle, and sometimes being 'just like everybody else' in appearance meets a young person's need to conform in a relatively harmless fashion. Parents should be aware, however, that certain fashions and hairstyles may signal membership in adolescent groups that could involve a host of other characteristics. There is no substitute for parents' good judgment, based upon an informed knowledge of what goes on in the schools and knowledge of their children's friends.

There is also value in having children wait until a certain age to do certain things, such as dating or getting one's ears pierced or spending the night at a friend's house. Looking forward to these rites of passage can be a positive experience. Many parents find that working out some common agreements with the parents of their children's friends is a helpful approach. Otherwise, some of these decisions may be overly influenced by peer pressure, with children participating in adult-type activities at earlier and earlier ages—second-graders wearing nylons or sixth-graders dating, for example. Wing plans should preserve a child's right to childhood as well as prepare the child for adulthood.

The purpose of wing plans is to help parents gradually transfer responsibility to a child by recognizing that growth and relinquishment are achieved over time on a step-by-step basis. Such plans also keep parents actively involved in helping their children achieve the competence that responsibility and freedom require. Parents are *in it together* for and with their children. Three additional illustrations of areas in which wing plans could be developed are household chores, money and jobs, and school work.

Household Chores. How kids help out around the house or do *not* seems to be one of parent's most frequent complaints. How many times have parents said:

"Not only is her room a mess, but she likes it that way."

"They never clean up after themselves."

"He doesn't seem to feel any responsibility for taking care of things around the house."

"How can I get my kids to help out?"

Of course, children's perspectives often differ from their parents. I recall my sister sharing her frustration at trying to put into effect a new system for children's chores at her house. Her son spoke for his siblings when he complained, "But we don't *like* working." Most kids don't, and it is unreasonable for parents to expect that children will always do their jobs cheerfully with no grumbling. (This may be equivalent to our son's definition of a wimp: "Someone who likes school so much that he's disappointed when the bell rings.") It is *not* unreasonable, however, for parents to expect and require that children—in ways that are appropriate to their age and abilities—do their part to contribute to the household. Children may not like it, but they can appreciate that jobs need to be done, and it is only fair for everybody to help. This is especially true when parents begin to communicate this expectation to their children from an early age. Jobs should be perceived as necessary contributions to the family, not as punishments.

A toddler can be expected, for example, to help Mom or Dad pick up his toys. Later he can do it for himself. A preschooler may set the table as well as pick up her toys. By the time a child is in elementary school, parents might add taking out the trash and clearing the table to the list of chores. And older children might begin helping with jobs such as sweeping, laundry, food preparation, snow shoveling, and yard work. Friends of ours prepared their children so well that their senior daughter, sophomore son, and junior-high daughter held down the homefront for three entire weeks while the parents were out of the country. (This was done, of course, with ample support from friends and neighbors.) One daughter did confess that at one point she had "to wash a pan before fixing supper," but imagine the parents delight upon their return to find the house in decent shape and a welcome-home dinner prepared. Parents who expand job responsibilities as children grow older are preparing them for independent living. They are also communicating their confidence.

Parents must be flexible, however. There are such things as unrealistic expectations, and some parents treat their children like hired help. The purpose in having children help is not for them to do all the work, but for them to do enough of it that they appreciate that household chores are a shared responsibility. Adolescents frequently have extremely demanding work, study, and activity schedules. School for them is often equivalent to a job for an adult, and parents must build into the system not only some flexibility but a degree of grace as well. Time lines for accomplishment can be set generously. Certain jobs (although obviously not the dishes) can be done anytime Thursday, Friday, or Saturday, for example. Jobs may be traded off among the children, at their initiation and agreement, or Mom and Dad may even pitch in and do the children's chores during final exam week.

Certain jobs tend to be cooperative, such as doing dishes, and children can be involved in the decision-making process which results in the distribution of these tasks. Other chores are the individual's responsibility which can be developed into a wing plan.

Sharing household chores builds on the first two family strength areas discussed in this book. Not only are parents helping move the child along the continuum from parental control to self-control, but they are reinforcing cohesiveness. And parents' confidence also reinforces a child's self-esteem. The child learns that *I can do it! I am important! I am needed!* Once in a while, a child may even surprise his parents and say, in an incredulous tone, "Do you know that Johnny Smith doesn't even know how to operate a vacuum cleaner?"

Money and Jobs. A second area in which many parents have difficulty teaching self-responsibility is money management. Most of us have heard or felt the frustration expressed in the following parental laments:

"My kids think of me as an endless source of money."

"My daughter never saves a dime. She sees her allowance simply as money to blow."

"My son wouldn't think of wearing the same brand tennis shoes I wear. His cost three times more, and he can't understand my reluctance to simply shell out the money."

Or Bill Cosby's TV complaint:

"Theo, I don't have a $96.00 shirt, and I have a job."

What many parents don't appreciate is the connection between how they think of and communicate their role as providers and the values and expectations reflected in these comments. There appears to be a consumer mentality which equates being parents with providing not only for children's needs but their wants as well. And these wants can be endless. One need only reflect on the explosion of options available in our lives to appreciate the problem. If one designer shirt makes a child feel good, wouldn't five more make him feel even better? Some parents buy into this mentality. They seem eager to spare their children the discomfort of being different. They overcompensate and over-indulge. What one white sport coat did for a teenager's self-image in the 1950s takes about five pairs of designer tennis shoes to accomplish today. Some parents may even substitute purchases for expressions of affection or commitments of time.

When young people grow up in neighborhoods and attend schools where this definition of parental providing is common, is it any wonder that children enter adulthood with the expectation that they should start out at the same level at which their parents have finally arrived? They have been conditioned, often with amazing sacrifices on their parents' part, to expect that they are owed or entitled to a certain lifestyle—from designer clothes to sports cars to colleges with big price tags. Many young people feel little responsibility to contribute to this process themselves.

Many parents breathe a sigh of relief when their teenager shows enough initiative to get a part-time job, only to discover that the teen views the money he earns as he had earlier viewed his allowance. Adolescents increasingly use the money they earn from part-time jobs for luxury purchases—CD players, cars, or expensive clothes. One young man we know earned three thousand dollars at a summer job, but half of that amount went to finance two parties. Some people even suggest that adolescents who have part-time jobs are more likely to have problems with alcohol and drug abuse. One explanation, of course, is the extra money. Another is the expansion of contacts beyond the ordinary high-school environment. Another concern about adolescents working is the effect a part-time job might have on a student's academic performance. For some students, the time might be better spent earning high enough grades to become eligible for scholarships. A part-time job can be productive and valuable when the teen is expected to use some of the earned money for needs as well as wants—saving for college or a car, for example.

Even when parents can afford to meet all the expectations their children and society seem to be thrusting upon them, they are not doing their children any favors by indiscriminately granting every wish and desire. Rather, such indulgence encourages a value system that confuses luxuries with necessities and needs with wants. Over-indulgent parents also condition children with the expectation that the greatest satisfactions in life come from increasingly expensive purchases or experiences.

Perhaps parents need to rethink what it means to be good providers, not only for their own benefit but for their children's. In a world of diminishing resources, shouldn't parents be teaching stewardship instead of exploitation? In a world where millions of people go to sleep in great need of life's essentials, should parents be raising children to worry about nothing but their own personal pleasure? This area—money and its use and management—challenges families to re-examine their values as world citizens.

A wing plan in the area of money might include a small child setting aside a percentage of his allowance for future savings. The child then sees some responsibility for picking up the tab on his own future. This amount might increase as the child grows older, with additional money contributed to savings from part-time jobs. A percentage of the child's allowance might also be set aside for a contribution to a church with an active mission program or to some other philanthropic organization. One family we know decided when the children were teenagers to share the support of a child abroad. It often helps if children can see a direct connection between what they give and how it helps others. We recently read an article about the influence of his parents' teaching on Martin Luther King, Jr. The Kings taught their children that money earned should be dispersed in thirds: one-third to save, one-third to spend, and one-third to share with others.[7]

Children can also be expected to save their own money for special purchases, perhaps paying a percentage of a new bike or a pair of athletic shoes. Adolescents can help offset the cost of yearbooks or school rings with money earned from babysitting or paper routes. Older adolescents can be expected to save some money for college.

Parents can help older children learn money management skills by sharing with them some of the complexities of budgeting, insurance rates, and credit shopping. All of these issues need to be discussed and considered as parents develop wing plans for their children to learn not only how to earn and manage money but also how to conscientiously assume the responsibility that comes with its possession.

Schoolwork and Homework. In years past, when certain experts suggested that school and homework should be the exclusive domain of the child, parents were all too willing to listen. Helping a child do homework didn't seem to fit in well with the popular concept of quality time anyway. Many teachers welcomed the opportunity for increased autonomy in the classroom, and it seemed as if schools were embarking on a path which would result in children becoming academically responsible. What many parents and educators failed to appreciate was the fact that the value of study and learning isn't something that children learn automatically or effortlessly. It must be learned with patience, practice, and sometimes prodding. For children whose earliest schooling was entertainment ("Sesame Street," for example), it was easy to conclude that *all* learning should be fun, and they didn't develop the perseverance to stick with the work when it became either difficult or boring.

Wing plans in schoolwork and homework need to be tailored not only to each child and family but often to each school as well. Some children are self-motivated and academically mature enough that they *are* able to own most of their homework from a fairly early age. Most children, however (we had at least two in this category), require at least periodic parental intervention and encouragement. Some children are able to complete much of their homework on school time; others need to bring classwork as well as assignments home. Some schools make few homework demands on their pupils (although the findings of recent national reports on education are reversing this situation). Other schools are like the elementary school our children attended. The teachers gave so much homework that at times the children's schoolwork structured much of our family time. Our daughter had more homework in fifth and sixth grades than we'd had in high school.

The educational support needed by individual children will also vary depending on each child's intellectual maturity, interests, and attention span. Even bright students may not have the organizational and follow-through skills to enable them to complete school assignments successfully. As educators pay more attention to the different ways in which children learn, parents and teachers have been able to respond better to some of these differences.

Keeping in mind that educational wing plans will vary from child to child, home to home, and school to school, here are some general suggestions parents can apply to help move their children along the continuum from dependence to self-responsibility:

Read yourself, and read together for fun. Not only is reading a strong cohesive activity to be enjoyed in families with children of all ages, but it is one of the best preparations for school.

Talk to and with your child. Answer questions. Visit museums, zoos, historic sites, and parks together. Go on outings where you are not only available to respond to questions but to learn alongside your child. A vacation at the ocean might prompt, for example, a trip to the library to find books on sea shells or pelicans.

Be interested in what your child is doing in school. This includes games played at recess as well as classroom subjects, the names of friends as well as homework assignments. Respond to and encourage the interests your child expresses. Parents might rent videos that build on what the child is learning in school. When our youngest son studied the Soviet Union in junior high, we all watched *Dr. Zhivago.*

Don't push. You want your child to see your interest as a response to his and not as a manipulation to get him to do what pleases you.

Be involved in your child's school. Know the teachers. Attend back-to-school nights, and be aware of the school's strengths and weaknesses. When a problem occurs, help your child's teachers understand your child's specific needs and strengths. Explore together what both of you can do to help your child learn and succeed.

Don't let a test tell you who your child is. Remember that a test is only a clue or indicator, one piece of academic evidence to help you and your child better understand strengths and weaknesses. A child's home background, motivation, and interests are more often better indicators of future success than test scores.

Help with homework. Homework poses a dilemma. Parents want to encourage and support their children's academic progress, but they do not want to feel responsible for their children's homework. One of our friends is fond of telling about her daughter's first book report in the third grade. Because the daughter was not yet reading well, her mother began by reading the chosen book to her. Then the daughter did not have the slightest idea how to write a book report, so her mother wrote one out and gave it to the girl to copy. "I wouldn't have minded," confessed our friend, "except that when she brought the paper home, the teacher had given her a C." Achieving a balance between helping too much and not helping enough is a challenge for parents as well as teachers. What, then, are some ways that parents can help with homework?

First, structure time for homework. Family rules and routines can provide for a time, place, and opportunity to do homework.

Keep track of assignments on a calendar. By the time children reach junior high, they should have their own calendars to post assignments. Helping children learn to pace their work is one of the most helpful contributions a parent can make.

Help the child learn how to study. A parent can help a child learn different ways of studying for different kinds of assignments and tests. A vocabulary test in which the teacher asks for the definition is studied for differently from one in which the teacher provides the definitions and expects the students to write in the words. An essay test require different skills than a short-answer test.

A parent can read a social studies or science chapter with a child, alternating paragraphs. After each section, parent and child can discuss what was important about that section, which will help the child learn what to look for when reading. Individual wing plans will vary, but the investment of time, energy, and encouragement will always be worth it.

The process of moving children along the continuum from dependence to self-discipline is not smooth. There are setbacks and detours, and parents cannot always see progress. The investments made in caring, sharing, and relating can help parents and children weather the disappointments. The process takes both patience and persistence, but the payoff is not only for the family. It is also for the children, who will arrive at adulthood better equipped to make the most of their strengths and gifts because they have learned self-control.

When our oldest son was fifteen, he invited a school friend to spend the weekend with us. It was a special time for Chris, and we all enjoyed his friend's company. The following Monday evening, the phone rang, and it was Chris's friend wanting to come over and play some after-school football with our sons. Chris asked me if this would be all right, and I reminded him of the history test he had the next day. He started to explain to his friend on the phone, then stopped and took another try at persuading me to change my mind. I reaffirmed our family policy of homework before play on school nights and suggested that Chris's friend might come over another afternoon. Of course, the friend wanted to come at that moment, and Chris would have much preferred playing football to studying for a history test. The friend must have said something like, "But I thought your Mom was so nice," and Christopher answered, "Yes, but sometimes she has to be the bad guy." When I looked up, he caught my eye and winked, and I knew that—at least in that situation and at that moment—he understood. For all parents there are times when love must be tough. An unknown author wrote this dramatic illustration:

> *I loved you enough to ask where you were going, with whom and at what time you would be home.*
>
> *I loved you enough to insist that you save your money and buy a bike for yourself, even though we could afford to buy one for you.*
>
> *I loved you enough to be silent and let you discover that your new best friend was a creep.*
>
> *I loved you enough to make you take a candy bar back to the drugstore (with a bite out of it) and tell the clerk, "I stole this yesterday and want to pay for it."*
>
> *I loved you enough to stand over you for two hours while you cleaned your room, a job that would have taken me fifteen minutes.*
>
> *I loved you enough to let you see anger, disappointment, and tears in my eyes. Children must learn that their parents are human.*
>
> *I loved you enough to let you assume the responsibility for your actions even when the penalties were so harsh they almost broke my heart.*
>
> *But most of all, I loved you enough to say no when I knew you would hate me for it. Those were the most difficult battles of all. I'm glad I won them, because in the end, you won something, too.*

What the child wins is the opportunity to learn self-control because the parents are the leaders in the home. It is precisely those parents who are willing to exercise control when the behavior of the child and the values of the family require it whose leadership is most likely to be accepted as a matter of course. When it is clear who is in charge, the parent is then able to relinquish responsibility to the growing child, and the child learns self-discipline when given encouragement and accountability, practice and protection, the roots of support and the wings of freedom.

5

Affiliation: Who Can Help?

When the sea was calm all boats alike
Showed mastership in floating.
William Shakespeare
Coriolanus 4.1.6–7

Strong families develop and sustain a network of relationships with other individuals, groups, and institutions outside the home. These relationships provide the opportunity for participation, a sense of identification, the assurance of support, and the perspective of association and involvement.

Smooth Sailing and Rough Seas

Although all the storms we experience in life are not of equal magnitude, some may require of us a reserve of resources not always needed when seas are calm. The roots families nurture to help compensate for losses, adapt to changes, or cope with stress not only reflect their strength but help define it. This is true whether a crisis results from some contemporary temptation, the inevitable transitions of family life, or the unusual circumstances only some must face. Why do the same problems that strengthen some families break others apart? Why do some families fold under even minor pressures and others overcome extreme adversity with grace? These questions do not lend themselves to easy answers. More and more, however, families are acknowledging the positive role that relationships outside the family play in helping them cope when the going gets rough.

114

Individuals and families who have developed these ongoing outside relationships find that the channels of support and communication are already available to them—to help cope with both daily stresses and major crises. When psychologist George S. Everly, Jr., designed a stress test for the U.S. Department of Human Services, he included good family and social relationships as strong, positive factors in an individual's stress-coping capacity. His research instrument allows one to record and total positive and negative points based upon such factors as health and exercise habits, relaxation techniques, weight, and workload. Out of a perfect score of 115, a person can earn 20 positive points for having a supportive family and a social activity with a group that meets at least once a month.[1]

Supportive relationships, however, require an investment of time and a conscious commitment to expand the family's activities to include other families, groups, or organizations. Close ties aren't the product of osmosis. Families must intentionally work at developing these relational roots. And they must encourage growing children who are learning to use their wings to do so also.

WHO ARE OUR MODELS?

In the past, extended families were often taken for granted. New couples settled near their relatives. They belonged to neighborhood churches, joined organizations they had known about since childhood, sent their children to schools they had attended, and were able to rely—with little effort and less resolution—on a natural network of support, friendship, and communication.

Mobility, work schedules, and changing lifestyles have altered this situation dramatically. For many families who live in suburban housing developments or urban apartment complexes, it is possible to remain anonymous despite geographic proximity to thousands of other people. Because families are less motivated by loneliness than single individuals, they may not find the time, inclination, and encouragement to establish close relationships outside the home. Although individual family members may find friends in school or at work, families do not share many relationships in common. With little outside support to help a family adjust to inevitable transitions, overcome difficulties, or even put pressures into perspective, the problems the family encounters can become overwhelming, with the marriage failing or the family falling apart. No person need face life alone, and neither should families, although isolation seems to be becoming more common than its opposite.

A young mother wrote to Ann Landers wondering what had happened to the support system that used to exist in all families? She recalled that her grandmother had come when her mother's four children were born, and an elder sister had moved in to help an aunt recover from surgery. When her own baby was born, however, her mother advised her to hire a nurse, and her husband's mother explained that she couldn't leave her job. Even her neighbors turned her down. The young mother and her husband coped as best they could with the strains of a new baby. Ann's response emphasized that, although we may be paying a high price for the demise of a sense of family, times have indeed changed.

This breakdown of the extended-family support system has had a critical impact on minority populations where elaborate family networks existed in the past. In American Indian communities, for example, children have traditionally been considered a communal responsibility, but family networks are fast disappearing as many American Indians must leave their homes to find employment in cities. Teachers in urban schools that serve American Indian children tell of a sharp increase in the number of homeless children who have no sense of identity or belonging.

In the past, urban African-American families were often held together by an informal partnership between African-American churches and the extended family. Now they frequently find themselves with almost no viable support and few models for success. Many middle-class African-American families have moved to the suburbs, leaving behind the terrifying cycle of teenage parenthood, unemployment, drug and alcohol abuse, and violence.[2]

FAMILY TIES

When relatives are available to provide love and support, families are indeed fortunate, but families must also reach beyond their relatives to other relationships of friendship and support, even when family ties are well-functioning and positive. These other relationships may be formed with friends, neighbors, or co-workers. Often what is important is not the counsel, encouragement, or helping hand but simply the knowledge that friends are there if they are needed. Epicurus reminds us: "It is not so much our friends' help that helps us as the confidence of their help." A couple we knew developed a friendship with a single, professional woman who worked in the same office as one of them. She was included in many of the family's activities, and during the holidays the two young sons visited in her apartment to help trim her Christmas tree. This relationship was beneficial not only for the single woman, who experienced life through a child's perspective, but also for the children, who had yet another adult who cared about them and was deeply concerned for their well-being.

These close ties with extended family, friends, co-workers, and neighbors are valuable because they are formed with people who truly care and have made an emotional investment in others. It is this emotional content that leads most people to turn to friends and family rather than professional helpers when they need help.

CHURCH TIES

Churches are another source of outside support for many families. When James Michener was interviewed about his views on the "rocky, exciting eighties,"[3] he was asked what he would do were he a young man starting out in a new town. Michener remarked that the first thing he would do was "affiliate with some good church because I would be more likely to find someone with my own set of values." Michener expressed something that he and many others have authenticated in their own lives about the value of churches, synagogues, and other religious institutions in providing support for families and individuals.

In a study conducted by family researchers David Olson and Hamilton McCubbin to determine how families cope, there were five major coping strategies identified by the twelve hundred families participating. Among these strategies, seeking spiritual support was considered the most important. Valued by both husbands and wives throughout the family life cycle, seeking spiritual support meant that these families "sought advice from ministers, attended church services, participated in church activities, and had faith in God."[4] Spiritual resources and support contribute to maintaining the family unit and individual self-esteem in dealing with problem situations.

In another study, researcher Jerry Lewis teamed up with John G. Looney to compare and contrast competent working-class African-American families with competent affluent African-American families. The authors discovered that the differences were not nearly as great as one might expect. While acknowledging the need for additional research into economic implications, they pointed out that the most competent working-class families were very much like the most competent affluent families. In both instances, "Religion was a central aspect of family life for the competent families, whereas such was not the case for the least competent families." Lewis and Looney pointed out: "It is well to emphasize that the mental health professions as a group may underestimate the adaptive value of religious beliefs and activities."[5] Furthermore, there is a striking correlation between church membership and a significantly lower rate of divorce. Religious commitment is important not only because of the strength families derive from the content of their beliefs and commitment to their faith, but also because churches help reinforce values by providing positive and supportive social pressure on the family unit. Church and family, therefore, often see themselves as partners in the struggle to resist the tide of negative values prevailing in society.

Many churches have become very intentional about the structures and programs they sponsor to help families. The Mormons, for example, encourage members to hold weekly family-at-home nights, a time together which includes some spiritual instruction, some sharing, and some fun. Mormon churches traditionally offer a wide range of activities (both social and spiritual) for all ages and stages. Catholic churches often use Saturday school as a vehicle to influence children's and families' values as part of their religious instruction. A Jewish temple established *huvurah* (or friendship) groups to help blend support and control for member families. In the 1970s, Foundry United Methodist Church, an inner-city congregation in Washington, D.C., discovered that it was losing families to suburban churches. The Family Ministries committee began developing support for a comprehensive program of intergenerational activities that included family camping, ice cream socials, holiday workshops, square dances, and picnics, as well as an adult church school class that addressed family concerns and issues. Not only did this program help increase family membership at the church, but—surprisingly—it also attracted singles and older adults. "What we discovered," observed Luise Gray, Family Ministries coordinator at that time, "is that families, singles, and older adults need to interact and support each other and that the program which best supported families helped establish needed intergenerational ties for all."

Writing for Howard University's Institute for Urban Affairs and Research on the support mechanisms in African-American communities, Lawrence Gary made a similar discovery. Citing churches as one of three significant supports within the African-American community (kinship bonds and voluntary organizations being the other two), he uses St. Paul's AME in Washington, D.C., as an example. The church had more than twenty-five different organizations giving children and adults opportunities to relate and interact—including youth choirs, Boy Scouts, the young people's department, junior ushers, junior stewards, trustee helpers, and Sunday school classes. To reinforce the importance of the African-American church, Gary quoted a book on the African-American family by Robert Staples. "The Black church," Staples maintained, "has acted as a tension reduction mechanism . . . given credence to the cultural heritage of black people, validated their worth, and provided them hope for the future."[6] Churches everywhere are becoming more intentional about developing structures to help families.

COMMUNITY TIES

Voluntary organizations also meet some of the support needs of families. Because most of these groups have some other primary reason for being, family support is usually an unanticipated secondary advantage to membership. It is certainly not an inevitable benefit, but the real possibility exists that a wide range of voluntary groups can help support families. These include community, social, neighborhood, educational, philanthropic, and special-interest groups. Cooperatives organized to share babysitting or pool shopping resources, for example, may develop into family support systems. Sports or academic interests may also bring individuals together in an informal network of family support. We know a group of people who attended a YMCA summer camp more than a decade ago and discovered that they shared so many common interests and values that they have continued to attend the same family camp every year in addition to keeping in touch during the year.

Educational institutions can also create opportunities to support families. Several elementary schools in our area sponsor family activities that are designed as nothing more than opportunities for families to have fun together. A dramatic example of this kind of support was in the context of an American Indian Pow Wow at an Indian school in Seattle, Washington. The event was attended and enjoyed by people of all ages — from two-year-olds and young adults to grandparents with whole families coming to participate in the socializing and dancing. The activity also helped to reinforce cultural rituals with a ceremonial opening and closing, and to alert community members to common concerns — hospitalizations, illnesses, births, and other news.

BUILDING BRIDGES

Extended family, friends, neighbors, co-workers, churches, schools, and voluntary organizations can all offer opportunities for families to develop close relationships. These informal networks are often far more useful to most people than formalized networks of support. Informal networks do not form automatically, however, and families — even healthy, well-functioning ones — must take the time to develop and cultivate these ties. Many social service agencies now work cooperatively with churches to help identify elderly and homebound people who need support. Family counselors not only urge clients to seek opportunities for affiliation on their own, but they may also, as a follow-up to counseling, actually create friendship groups or family clusters that continue after therapy is complete. We are familiar with a marriage enrichment program that resulted in numerous family support groups who continued to meet in the aftermath of the enrichment retreat.

A fascinating study of a program in Hawaii called *lima kokua* (or Helping Hands) suggests that the helping professions can take even more advantage of natural networks. That these networks can assist working parents with young children find and maintain daycare has already been demonstrated. This particular study, however, "pioneered a method for professionals to identify and recruit natural helpers in the community with the goal of alleviating or intervening in family stress that might otherwise lead to abuse or neglect." Natural networks that revolved around a central figure (or "gatekeeper") whose job it was to "act as an exchange agent or matchmaker for needs and resources and also to offer direct advice, support, and practical help to members of the network" were identified in each community.[7]

Programs such as Hawaii's Helping Hands experiment offer the promise of more partnerships between professional helpers and the informal support systems that already exist in communities. These partnerships could be an effective way of reaching people in need who are not now served by public- and private-sector agencies.

They've Got What We Need

Family Relationships

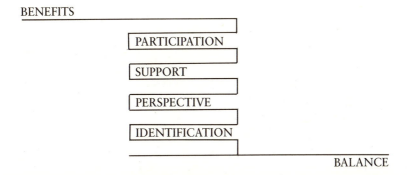

What benefits do relationships outside the home provide families? We have identified at least four: participation, support, perspective, and identification. Children who grow up in families whose roots provide these benefits will seek them for themselves as they develop their own wings and relate to others.

Participation

The first and most obvious benefit of outside relationships is that they provide families with opportunities to participate. Community groups, churches, service organizations, and other groups can become laboratories where children learn leadership and involvement.

Children, especially, may discover in these groups opportunities to take responsibility and receive recognition in ways not always available in schools. A boy or girl who might not qualify for the varsity soccer team at the middle school may be a strong addition to a community team. A student not nominated to serve on the school's student council may be elected as a leader in the church youth group or volunteer for its program committee. A member of the chorus in the annual high-school musical may win the lead in a community club's production. Outside groups and organizations often pay special attention to the importance of participation and recognition opportunities for its members, with positive pressure to become involved. A sixth-grade teacher at our church, for example, assigned a new set of class officers each month so that all the children in the class had an opportunity to learn the responsibilities (and experience the recognition) of being president, vice-president, secretary, and treasurer. In many groups, the only requirement for joining is a common concern or a shared interest. Outside organizations can actually provide opportunities equivalent to apprenticeships for children to learn group dynamics, public speaking, organizational and relational skills, cooperation and leadership skills. Such apprenticeships describe yet another avenue for helping our children along the roots-to-wings continuum. Through their models, institutional support, and personal encouragement outside organizations can become partners with the family and help children learn the skills necessary to relate to others and realize their potential. Furthermore, families who are active in such groups are important to the successful functioning of these groups. This feeling of belonging reinforces not only individual self-esteem, but also pride for all of a family's members.

Support

A second benefit of affiliation is support. Families as well as individuals need support. It is not a matter of *if* families will need the support of others but *when*. All families experience hard times, whether daily distresses or infrequent catastrophes, where the help, hope, and understanding of others is needed. Sometimes the support needed is tangible—information, a visit, a job tip, a recipe, a tool, a hug, a loan, or chicken soup. At other times, the support needed is intangible — listening, caring, sharing, encouraging, or modeling. One of the most significant supports others can offer is their model of how they have adapted to certain experiences, coped with crises, or learned from mistakes.

Both kinds of support, tangible and intangible, are relationship-dependent. Families best able to cope over time are those who are connected to a supportive network and who actively use this network to solve problems. The other key point to be made about support networks is that they are reciprocal. Families not only feel free to ask others for help, but others also feel free to come to them. They are not always on the receiving end, but they are also attentive to the needs and problems of others. Outside relationships teach us both how to receive help and how to give it.

Perspective

A third benefit for families of outside relationships is that they can help give perspective. It is all too easy for families to find their lives dominated by their problems. Like the poet John Keats, sometimes one needs to stand alone on the shore of the wide world "and think till love and fame to nothingness do sink." One of the skills shared by families who are strong and cope well is the ability to redefine a situation in manageable terms, to reframe a problem as something they can handle. This skill can give a family a feeling of control, a sense of confidence and hope. Other people, of course, can play a major role in helping families reframe problems. Their example and experience are a testimony to the fact that problems can be overcome. It is the experience of others that makes their advice and encouragement credible, their caring that makes it valued.

This insight into the importance of reframing partially explains the success of support groups organized to help families and individuals face life-threatening problems such as alcoholism, drug addiction, and even terminal illness. The fact that many of these groups consist of people who have experienced similar problems makes their help especially valuable. Such groups can help members anticipate not only the external events they might have to face, but also how they are likely to feel about what happens. Individuals who have already been through a crisis can provide a model of success, perseverance, or perhaps simply endurance. When they promise that time can heal, or that out of despair and death come new life, their experience makes their testimony credible.

Not only do families need perspective on their problems, both major and minor, but sometimes they also need to put their wants into perspective as well. Perhaps now more than ever, it is tempting for individuals and families to see themselves as the center of the universe, to be seduced into believing that living the good life is all that really matters. There is more to life than money and the things and experiences it buys. A self-gratifying lifestyle not only flys in the face of what most of the world's great religions teach, but it is the opposite of what makes families strong. Healthy families are involved in the world. They reach out to those in need and, in the process, develop a sensitivity to others and a strength of character that is reflected in all areas of their lives. Outside organizations and individuals can play positive roles in calling the needs of others to our attention and in providing structures through which we can respond. They can help us move beyond self-interest to a recognition of the need for interdependence. A family that is continually challenged to think of those who are hungry, homeless, or hurting finds it easier to keep its priorities in order. Members of such a family may be less inclined to take for granted the health and happiness they enjoy. They may even appreciate their own good fortune enough to want to share it with others. A gospel song reminds us: *For all that's made me happy and gave me reason to believe I want to put it back for all that I received.*[8]

A church with a strong mission program, for example, is a constant reminder that there is more to life than sports cars and hot tubs. A social service organization that offers us the opportunity to relate to disadvantaged children teaches that what we do in the present can shape the future. These organizations can help us gain a critical perspective on our wishes, wants, values, and goals, just as they can with our problems.

Of course, all good things can be taken to the extreme. We know of families in which the parents are so involved in social action or church work that they have practically no time for their children. Some individuals become so focused on a single issue that they sacrifice their sense of humor, their relationships, and even their joy in living to the cause. Others become so convinced that what is right for them is right for everybody that they look askance at anyone who doesn't believe what they believe or support what they support. Still others turn their own service and self-denial into self-righteousness, judging those who have made different decisions.

In his book on American parenting, Joseph Novello helps us understand the importance of keeping all aspects of our life in balance. His model for mental health places the hero on a "foundation of social interest" while he juggles "work, family, friends, self, love, personal philosophy, and religion."[9]

Each of us must discover the appropriate balance for our own lives, based upon our values and our unique gifts and skills along with the opportunities we have to use them in our work, our personal lives, our families, and our outside interests and commitments. These relationships of affiliation can help us find the balance.

Identification

It used to be that the definition of who we were as individuals rested upon who we were in families. For generations, individual identity incorporated a description of relational ties. Individuals were not only who they were by name, but also 'son of,' 'daughter of,' 'mother of,' 'brother of,' and so on. These relationships helped describe, even characterize, individuals. This situation has changed. Now many Americans define who they are in terms—not of family relationships—but professional or peer relationships. The cards in the billfold frequently tell the story. People are members of the business community, the academic community, the computer community, or the medical community. They think of themselves as government workers, city workers, or company workers. For many, this shift in emphasis has created confusion rather than clarity, challenging not only the sources of our personal identities, but undermining the importance of family identity as well. Even national identity is sometimes seen as a source of confusion as well as pride.

With the renewal of commitment to family, community, and country taking place today, many Americans have begun to question the assumptions of recent decades. Columnist Ellen Goodman wonders: "If our offices are our neighborhoods, if our professional lives are our new ethnic tags, then how do we separate ourselves from our jobs? Self-worth isn't just something to measure in the marketplace."[10] Its first measure is defined by our membership in a family. What does it mean to be an Allen, an Adamson, or an Alvarez? It means something to be Italian, Irish, Swiss, Hispanic, or Texan. It means something to be long-term friends with neighbors, co-workers, or fellow students. It means something to be a musical family, a camping family, a swimming family, a YMCA family, or a Capitol Heights Community Center family. It means something to be United Methodist, Mormon, Catholic, Jewish, Presbyterian, or Baptist. By joining such groups, a family both gives and receives meaning.

Families need to begin early to identify the individuals and groups who can help reinforce their values and provide friendship, support, identification, and opportunities for growth and service.

Ethnic cultures have long emphasized the need to give meaning and keep harmony in life. They recognize that this requires a balance between the various poles of our lives. Perhaps the time has come for others to learn this truth—that living harmoniously in the present is made possible when each finds a balance between relationships and self-reliance, altruism and personal achievement, tradition and innovation, loyalty and openness, the past and the future. How parents help children define this balance will help determine the strength of today's families. Families who invest in the *roots* of sharing, caring, teaching, and relating are providing a sound basis for the *wings* that enable children to become caring and competent adults. As the wise woman pointed out, this is the most valuable legacy we can leave to our children.

Discussion Questions _____

1. How would you complete the following statement: "Home is . . . ."
   a. about the family in which you were raised?
   b. about your own family?

2. What conflicts do you see between acceptance and accountability in the family? How has that been a problem in your home, or how have you resolved the tension?

3. What important changes affecting families have taken place in society? Which of these have made it more difficult for your family? Which have made it easier?

4. What do you think makes families strong?

5. What do you think is the difference between roots and wings?

6. Can you recall from your own growing-up years some of the roots in your home?

7. How did your parents encourage the development of wings?

8. What roots do you want to give your children?

9. How can you help your children acquire wings?

CHAPTER 2—COHESION: WHAT FAMILIES SHARE

1. What do members of your family have in common?

2. What activities do you enjoy as a family?

3. How often do you participate in the above activities?

4. What are some of your family's rituals and traditions? Which

are repeated from the past? Which have you discarded or adapted? Which have you invented or created?

5. Have any rituals evolved in your family that help you:
   a. celebrate good news?
   b. accept bad news?
   c. confront problems?
   d. reconcile differences?
   e. express affection?
   f. forgive or make up?

6. How have you planned so that your family can do things together?

7. List all the different hats you wear in order of importance to you. Which of these hats are essential? Which are dispensable?

8. What can different generations share with each other to help strengthen families?

9. Can you recall some of the stories, sayings, or legends you heard as a child?

10. How can you build flexibility into the practice of your family traditions?

11. What are some of the best times for talking with your family?

12. What kind of people do you want your children to become?

13. What are your values as a family? What rules do you have that support these values?

14. How much TV does your family watch? What programs do you watch? Individually? Together? Do you talk about what you watch?

15. What are some of your favorite family memories?

Strengthening Family Cohesion
A Worksheet

Choose a value (and the behaviors that support it) you would like to strengthen in your family.

Value _____

Behaviors _____

_____

1. What are some ways in which parents can model behaviors that support the value?

2. What are some ways in which the family as a whole can participate in behaviors that support the value?

3. How can parents reinforce individual behaviors that support the value?

4. What family rules can support the value?

5. Are there ways in which others (individuals, institutions) can support your family's goal in this value area?

CHAPTER 3 — AFFECTION: HOW PARENTS CARE

1. Complete the following statement as you think about each member of your family: "I appreciate in you . . . "

2. Tell *them.*

3. What are some everyday ways we can help family members feel good about themselves?

4. Think of each person in your family. What are some extraordinary things you can do to help each family member feel competent, confident, and worthwhile?

5. Think about the ways in which affection is expressed in your home. Which areas need more emphasis?
   - Touching?
   - Talking?
   - Doing?
   - Waiting?
   - Listening?
   - Laughing?
   - Forgiving?

6. What are some surprises you think each family member might appreciate?

7. What are some of your family's 'location jokes'?

8. Describe the rituals of reconciliation you have developed in your family. Have you observed any in other families?

CHAPTER 4 — CONTROL: WHY PARENTS TEACH

1. Are you pleased with your present parental leadership? If so,

why? If not, why not? What are the strengths and weak-nesses of your leadership?

2. What are the most common discipline problems you encoun-ter? What strategies do you use to handle these problems? What are your short-term goals in each case? Long-term goals?

3. Can you identify a specific situation in which your long-term goal was affirmed?

4. Review the values worksheet on pages 128–29. How do your family's rules reinforce its values?

5. What decisions would you list under each of the following headings?

Parent Decisions　　　Child Decisions　　　Shared Decisions

_____

_____

_____

_____

How does this list change as a child grows older?

6. What are some wing plans to help you transfer responsibility to a growing child?

7. What kinds of problems and concerns might prompt you to seek outside help (counseling, for example) for your family?

CHAPTER 5 — AFFILIATION: WHO CAN HELP

1. Make a list of the friends your family as a whole enjoys.

2. How have these friends helped your family in the past? How have you helped them?

3. What are some problems your family has faced for which you sought the support, encouragement, and counsel of oth-ers? What advice can others give who have faced the same or similar problems?

4. What kinds of support does your church provide for families and individuals facing difficulties such as parenting prob-lems, teen difficulties, school concerns, illness, drug or alco-

hol use, two-career stresses, single-parent concerns, divorce adjustments, empty-nest challenges, death, and so on?

5. How do your relationships of affiliation with individuals and/or organizations provide your family with opportunities for identification, support, perspective, and participation?

Notes _____

CHAPTER 1

1. Examples include affordable, quality daycare, after-school care, or part-time and shared jobs for parents, and so on.

2. *Beyond Rhetoric: A New American Agenda for Children and Families*, Final Report of the National Commission on Children: Washington, D.C. (U.S. Government Printing Office, July 1991), 18.

3. *Beyond Rhetoric*, 18–19.

4. *Beyond Rhetoric*, 19.

5. *Beyond Rhetoric*, 24.

6. *Beyond Rhetoric*, 21.

7. *Beyond Rhetoric*, 22.

8. Judy Mann, "Choices," *The Washington Post*, September 12, 1984. The Washington Post, 1984. Used by permission.

9. *Research on Successful Families*. A Report on a Conference Sponsored by the Office of the Assistant Secretary for Planning and Evaluation, U.S. Department of Health and Human Services (May 10, 1990). Compiled by Maria Krysan, Kristin A. Moore, and Nicholas Zill of Child Trends, 2100 M Street, N.W., Suite 610, Washington, D.C. 20037.

10. *Beyond Rhetoric*, 251.

11. Harold Kushner, *When All You've Ever Wanted Isn't Enough* (New York: Summit Books, 1986), 94. Used by permission.

12. O. Dean Martin, *Good Marriages Don't Just Happen* (Old Tappan-Fleming H. Revel Company, 1984).

13. Sylvia Ann Hewlett, "Watching a Generation Waste Away," *Time*, August 26, 1991, 10–12.

14. Ellen Goodman, "Parents Overwhelmed By the Culture," *The Washington Post*, August 17, 1991, A-21. © *The Washington Post*, 1991.

15. Kate Keating, "How is Work Affecting American Families?" *Better Homes and Gardens* magazine, vol. 66, February 1982, 32.

© Meredith Corporation, 1982. All rights reserved. Used by permission.

16. *Research on Successful Families.*

17. *Research on Successful Families,* 4.

18. *Research on Successful Families,* 4.

CHAPTER 2

1. *Sally Forth,* by Greg Howard (News American Syndicate: Field Enterprises, 1982).

2. Dan Sperling, "Close-up: Family Traditions," *USA Today,* December 6, 1984, 5D. © *USA TODAY,* 1984. Reprinted with permission.

3. Fyodor Dostoyevsky, *The Brothers Karamazov,* trans. Constance Garnett (New York: Random House, 1933), 819–20.

4. Letty Cottin Pogrebin, "How to Talk While Eating," *Ms. Magazine,* November 1981, 20. Used by permission.

5. Barrie S. Greiff, "Trade-Offs–Balancing Personal, Family, and Organizational Life," *Harvard Magazine,* May-June 1980, 48. Used by permission.

6. Pinocchio. © The Walt Disney Company. Used by permission.

7. William Raspberry, "Developing Character in Public Schools," *The Washington Post,* October 9, 1985, A-19. © 1985, The Washington Post Writers Group. Reprinted with permission.

8. Keith B. Richburg, "Teachers Want Emphasis on Character," *The Washington Post,* September 26, 1985, A-19. © 1985 *The Washington Post.* Used by permission.

9. Jay Mathews, "Teaching Values in U.S. Schools," *The Washington Post,* November 21, 1984. © *The Washington Post,* 1984. Used by permission.

10. Joseph R. Novello, *Bringing Up Kids American Style* (New York: A & W Publishers, Inc., 1981), chap. 1. Used by permission.

11. Thomas Lickonia, *Raising Good Children* (New York: Bantam Books, 1983), 350. Used by permission.

12. Ibid., 22.

CHAPTER 3

1. Normal M. Lobsenz, "Secrets of Giving and Getting More Emotional Support," *Woman's Day,* September 20, 1977, 148. © 1977 by CBS Magazines, the Consumer Publishing Division of CBS, Inc. Used by permission.

2. *A Nation at Risk,* National Commission on Excellence in Education, Washington, D.C., April 1983.

3. Joanna Tyler, "Young Children Need Freedom to Play," *The Bowie Blade News*, May 30, 1985, 11.

4. *CATHY*, by Cathy Guisewite (Universal Press Syndicate, February 13, 1986).

5. "Kids Under Construction," words by Gloria Gaither and Gary S. Paxton, music by William J. Gaither and Gary S. Paxton. © 1978 by William J. Gaither and Christian Grit Music Press. All rights reserved. Also, © 1978 by Christian Grit Music Press/ASCAP and Gaither Musica/ASCAP. All rights reserved. International copyright secured. Used by permission of Gaither Copyright Management and the Zondervan Music Group, Nashville.

CHAPTER 4

1. J. B. Stockdale, "Taking Stock," *Naval War College Review*, May-June 1979, 2. Used by permission.

2. Jerry M. Lewis, *How's Your Family?* (New York: Brunner/Mazel, Inc., 1979), 87–88.

3. In some models, this saving-up of feelings has been compared to collecting trading stamps that are later redeemed for prizes. In other models, it is called *gunny sacking*.

4. Carol Tavris, *Anger: The Misunderstood Emotion* (New York: Simon and Schuster, 1982), 127–28, 145. © 1982 by Carol Tavris. Reprinted by permission of Simon and Schuster, Inc.

5. From a discussion on discipline problems with at-risk students, Prince George's County, Maryland, August 1991.

6. Kahlil Gibran, *The Prophet* (New York: Alfred A. Knopf, 1943), 18.

7. William Raspberry, "The Awesome Influence of Fathers," *The Washington Post*, June 21, 1992, C-7.

CHAPTER 5

1. Sally Squires, "Learning to Live with Stress," *The Washington Post*, April 9, 1986, Health Section. © 1986, *The Washington Post*. Used by permission.

2. Lynne Duke, "Black Economic Disparity Deepened During 1980s," *The Washington Post*. August 9, 1991, A-244.

3. James Michener, quotes from "Interview–the 80's a Rocky Exciting Time," *U.S. News and World Report*, February 4, 1980, 41–42. © 1980, *U.S. News and World Report*. Used by permission.

4. David Olson and Hamilton McCubbin, *Families–What Makes Them Work* (Beverly Hills: Sage Publications, 1983), 147–48. Used by permission.

5. Jerry Lewis and John Looney, *The Long Struggle* (New York: Brunner/Mazel, 1983), 139 and 112. © Brunner/Mazel, 1983. Used by permission.

6. Lawrence E. Gary, *Support Systems in Black Communities: Implications for Mental Health Services for Children and Youth* (Washington, D.C.: McGraw Hill Book Company, Howard University Institute for Urban Affairs and Research, 1978), 29. Used by permission.

7. Eunice L. Watson and H. Collins, "Natural Helping Networks in Alleviating Family Stress," *The Annals of the American Academy of Political Science*, May 1982, 102–4. Used by permission.

8. "Put Something Back," by Joe Huffman and Aaron Wilburn. © 1981, Meadowgreen Music Co./BMG Songs, Inc., adm. by Meadowgreen Group, 54 Music Square E., Suite 305, Nashville, TN 37203/ BMG Songs, Inc., a member of BMG Music Publishing. International copyright secured. All rights reserved. Used by permission.

9. Joseph Novello, *Bringing Up Kids American Style* (New York: A. W. Publishers, 1986), 11. Used by permission.

10. Ellen Goodman, "You Are What You Do," *The Washington Post*, 1984. © 1984, The Boston Globe Newspaper Company/ Washington Post Writers Group. Used by permission.

Suggested Readings

Blankenhorn, David, Steven Bayme, and Jean Bethke Elshtain. *Rebuilding the Nest—A New Commitment to the American Family*. (Wisconsin: Family Services America, 1990.)

Curran, Dolores. *Traits of a Healthy Family*. (Minneapolis: Winston Press, Inc., 1983).

Hamburg, David. *Today's Children: Creating a Future for a Generation in Crisis*. (New York: Time-Life Books, 1992.)

Hewlett, Sylvia Ann. *When the Bough Breaks: The Cost of Neglecting Our Children*. (New York: Basic Books, 1991.)

Lickonia, Thomas. *Educating for Character—How Our Schools Can Teach Respect and Responsibility*. (New York: Bantam Books, 1991.)

Olson, David H., and Meredith Kilmer Hensen, editors. *Preparing Families for the Future*. (Minneapolis: National Council on Family Relations, 1990.)

Satir, Virginia. *peoplemaking*. (Palo Alto: Science and Behavior Books, Inc., 1972.)

Stinnett, Nick, and John DeFrain. *Secrets of Strong Families*. (Boston: Little, Brown, and Company, 1985.)